Please return or renew this item by the
last date shown. There may be a
charge if you fail to do so. Items can be
returned to any Westminster library.

Telephone: Enquiries 020 7641 1300
Renewals (24 hour service) 020 7641 1400
Online renewal service available.
Web site: www.westminster.gov.uk

Westminster Reference Library
35 St Martin's Street
London WC2H 7HP

City of Westminster

Twayne's Filmmakers Series

Warren French
EDITOR

Samuel Goldwyn

Samuel and Frances Goldwyn

Samuel Goldwyn

LAWRENCE J. EPSTEIN

Suffolk County Community College

BOSTON

Twayne Publishers

1981

Samuel Goldwyn

is first published in 1981 by Twayne Publishers,
A Division of G. K. Hall & Co.

Copyright © 1981 by G. K. Hall & Co.

Printed on permanent/durable acid-free paper and bound
in the United States of America

First Printing, November 1981

Library of Congress Cataloging in Publication Data

Epstein, Lawrence J. (Lawrence Jeffrey)
Samuel Goldwyn

(Twayne's filmmakers series)
Bibliography: pp. 174–76
Filmography: pp. 177–98
Includes index.
1. Goldwyn, Samuel, 1882–1974. I. Title. II. Series
PN1998.A3G643   791.43′0232′0924   81-4225
ISBN 0-8057-9282-1   AACR2

Contents

About the Author

Lawrence Jeffrey Epstein was born in New York City. He attended the State University of New York at Albany, receiving the B.A. and M.A. in English and the Ph.D. in philosophy and education. He also studied film history and filmmaking at Albany. During his early years of graduate study he starred in a number of experimental films and made several films himself.

Since 1974 Professor Epstein has been in the English Department at Suffolk County Community College in Selden, New York. In addition to courses in creative writing and journalism, he teaches a course there on mass media.

His fiction, reviews, and articles have appeared in a variety of publications. Besides popular culture, he has specialized in writing about Judaica.

Editor's Foreword

Since this multivolumed history of the cinema is organized on auteurist principles, most of the individual volumes deal with the work of an important director, especially directors who have also prepared their own scripts and produced their own films. Some volumes, however, will be devoted to other filmmakers, especially producers, who have exercised unusual influence on the final versions of their films, particularly their aesthetic qualities.

The producer has probably been the most maligned individual connected with filmmaking. Often conceived of as a tyrant with no taste or integrity, a contempt for the public and a fearful eye for censors, whose sole interest is in a fast buck, the producer has been the butt of many jokes and the target of frustrated players, directors, and writers. Often producers have fostered this stereotype by conceiving of themselves as the taskmasters who keep spendthrift directors, temperamental stars, and costume and set designers with delusions of grandeur in line in order to bring films in on schedule and within their budgets.

A handful of producers in this country and elsewhere, however, have conceived of filmmaking as an art rather than just a business and have sought to turn out a limited number of films, every detail of which they have supervised personally. They have specialized in films which have either extraordinary social or artistic merits or outstanding value as popular entertainment. In the United States, most of these producers were in the past associated with United Artists, a releasing company for a group of independent production units. United Artists was formed in 1919 by Mary Pickford, Douglas Fairbanks, Charles Chaplin, and D. W. Griffith, who wanted to keep for themselves the profits that others were making from their films.

Although Griffith was obliged to drop out of the association as his debts mounted, popular silent stars Pickford and Fairbanks and model auteur Chaplin continued to release their films through United Artists as long as they worked in this country.

Others joined them, though most of the newcomers were exclusively producers, not players or directors—principal among them were David O. Selznick, Walter Wanger, and Samuel Goldwyn. Even Darryl F. Zanuck's Twentieth Century organization briefly released its films through UA before merging with Fox Films under Zanuck's leadership.

United Artists reached the peak of its prestige in 1939–1940 when Chaplin released *The Great Dictator*, Goldwyn *Wuthering Heights*, Walter Wanger *The Long Voyage Home* from Eugene O'Neill's plays, and Selznick *Rebecca*, Alfred Hitchcock's first American film, even though Selznick's *Gone With the Wind* was distributed by Metro-Goldwyn-Mayer as part of a deal that enabled Selznick to borrow Clark Gable to play Rhett Butler.

Ironically, in an era when the kind of independent production United Artists pioneered has become a principal manner of making major films, the company—though its name still exists—is not an association of independent producers but part of a conglomerate. However, its contribution to keeping Hollywood filmmaking from degenerating into mindless mass production at the height of the power of the big studios in the 1930s and 1940s was unique and invaluable.

The distinctive qualities of Samuel Goldwyn's films cannot be easily summarized. It takes Lawrence Epstein the rest of this book to identify and explain "the Goldwyn touch." It should be cautioned here, however, that, because of the large number of films that Goldwyn produced during the thirty-six years that he controlled his own company, not every one of these productions—some of which are now lost, dated, or largely forgotten—is discussed, nor are those important and representative films chosen for detailed analysis discussed chronologically, although the arrangement is chronological within each chapter.

Professor Epstein has chosen instead to look at groups of films which are representative of Goldwyn's efforts to please a family public in his popular entertainment films starring comedians like Eddie Cantor, Bob Hope, and Danny Kaye, and to reach a concerned public often ignored by other producers and to educate them in problems of contemporary life in those serious dramas about domestic problems that are his chief claims to fame—*Street*

Scene, Arrowsmith, Cynara, These Three, Dead End, The Little Foes, and *The Best Years of Our Lives.* Only one other of his films competes with the last just named (Goldwyn's only Academy Award winner) as a film classic. Transcending both popular entertainment and domestic tragedy to become one of the few films to achieve truly mythical status, it is probably the film still most widely and admiringly associated with Goldwyn's name, *Wuthering Heights.*

Curiously, as Lawrence Epstein explains, Goldwyn came close to never making either *Wuthering Heights* or *The Best Years of Our Lives.* He lavished much more of his enthusiasm on such ill-fated projects as *Nana, The Goldwyn Follies,* and *Porgy and Bess.* Like all auteurs, he had his weaknesses, his prejudices, and his ill-advised pet projects. Whatever "the Goldwyn touch" was, it was no certain thing. But no Hollywood producer has established a better record than Goldwyn at his best. His story shows what a resolutely independent producer with an indomitable will could contribute to an industry constantly threatened with becoming mired in its complacent mediocrity. If only such a figure had had a comparable impact on television!

W. F.

Preface

A reporter once began a question posed to Samuel Goldwyn with the words "When Willy Wyler made *Wuthering Heights*. . . ." Goldwyn quickly interrupted him with "*I* made *Wuthering Heights*. Wyler only directed it."

Goldwyn's retort is more than an anecdote. In fact, it goes to the heart of explaining Samuel Goldwyn's long and extraordinary career as American film's most celebrated producer, a man who left a personal artistic stamp on every film that bore the legend "Samuel Goldwyn Presents."

The image of the Hollywood film producer as a fat, cigar-chomping ignoramus with a bloated belly, filled wallet, and vacant mind has so long been accepted by the American filmgoer (and even by some critics) that it has become a part of our cinematic folklore.

Producers fortunate enough to have been financially connected with artistically accomplished films are perceived to have made no artistic contributions to the films. Their contributions are thought to be limited to financial matters.

Because of this, few people conceive of a producer as a master-mind of film. That honor is relegated by tradition to the more obvious candidate, that last name on the opening credits, the director.

The reasons for the choice of director as artistic mastermind have long been established. All the great directors—Griffith, Eisenstein, Bergman, Truffaut, and a score of others—exercised their personal control over the artistic process in the way an author does with a good novel, or as a symphonic conductor with an important piece of music. Critics have always viewed films by one of these directors in the light of previous works by the same artist. Like a painting by Rembrandt or Chagall, Hitchcock's films are readily identifiable by his style and his technique. So it is even with films of inferior quality which parrot the Hitchcocks and the Carl Dreyers and the Frank Capras. It is the director, and no one else, who is granted the artistic accolades. The producer appears almost a ludicrous figure in comparison.

To place alongside the great directors the name of a producer would seem, then, an action akin to sacrilege. Yet there is one name that, by rights, belongs not merely alongside these others, but perhaps even on a plane above them. That man, that producer, was Samuel Goldwyn.

Goldwyn not only performed the functions for which the director has been credited, but he actually controlled all creative areas of the films he produced. Such diverse elements as writing, cinematography, and even makeup and set decoration were subject to his direct and all-encompassing control.

While other producers limited their interest in motion pictures to the bottom line of a balance sheet, Goldwyn, in a way unparalleled in the industry, sought to bring his imprint to all the movies he produced. He sought to produce a genuine work of art as he himself understood it.

The key to Goldwyn's success was his freedom. Goldwyn had no higher authority to which he felt, or was obliged to feel, responsible, and no other artistic conscience to salve. As an independent producer responsible for three or four films a year, Goldwyn could afford the luxury of total immersion in each of his projects. He could invest both capital and creative energy in equal measure. He could pick stories he thought important, and arrange to have the stories told without compromises, gimmicks, or shortcuts. To do the telling, he could draw on the finest talents available in the country. By limiting his output, he could concentrate on just those stories he really wanted to tell.

The idea of story is crucial in understanding Samuel Goldwyn's films. He saw characters not as sociological or psychological concepts but as real human beings in real situations dealing with believable and understandable social and psychological problems. He wanted his stories to transmit the drama of ordinary peoples' lives in times of stress and change. In short, the conflicts we all face at one point or another in our lives were crucial to Goldwyn.

He depended heavily on literary writers to write his screenplays and on adapting literary works to the screen precisely because he knew that at the center of all great literature was a story—a story filled with the real people and honest conflicts he needed for his films.

By selecting and refashioning the tales to be told, by carefully choosing his writers and collaborating with them, by visiting the set to make sure the director, the costume designer, and the others, did not vary from his vision, Goldwyn was able to produce story-oriented films of great technical mastery, films which, in time, prompted the admiring term "The Goldwyn Touch."

Despite Goldwyn's enormous contributions and the superior quality of many of his films, he has yet to be taken seriously in the works of film critics and film historians. Part of the reason for this attitude is the continuing stereotype of the producer-as-buffoon, and not a small measure to Goldwyn's own reputation as a purveyor of malapropisms. Virtually all the writing currently available about Samuel Goldwyn centers on humorous anecdotes of his life, recounting one or another of his supposedly frequent errors in English, errors commonly called "Goldwynisms."

I decided, therefore, that it was important to examine Goldwyn's career more closely than it had been done before. What needed to be written was an analysis of Goldwyn's films and an account of his contributions to the development of American film. This book, then, is the result of an attempt to right the mistaken image of Goldwyn and grant him his earned place in American film history.

In this book I intend to combine a thematic account of Goldwyn's work with an artistic account of Goldwyn's quest for quality, in particular how Goldwyn alone brought the concept of the "producer-auteur" to fruition. I will place special emphasis on Goldwyn's handling of mature subject matter, on films which express his passionate love of freedom, on his use of literary sources as the bases of so many of his films, on his use of musicals and comedies as the forms of light entertainment he provided for his audiences, and, finally, on his vision of America.

The principles involved in selecting which of Goldwyn's eighty independent productions to discuss (and, so, which to delete) were: (1) the importance of the film in understanding the stages of Goldwyn's career as a producer; and (2) the reception the film received. That is, all of Goldwyn's widely known films are discussed. It would take a much longer work to encompass all the films, but all those productions which I do not discuss at length could, I believe, fit comfortably into the general structure of Goldwyn's career provided in this book.

Preface

In writing this book I hope to explain and pass on Goldwyn's legacy: his emphasis on taste and his intrusion of an aesthetic conscience into the boardrooms of film corporations. I received substantial help in the preparation of this book from many people.

Dr. Warren French was responsible for suggesting Goldwyn as a subject to me and for providing crucial encouragement when it was needed. People at Audio Brandon Films were most helpful in providing films for viewing. All stills not otherwise credited were supplied by Movie Star News, in New York City. Carole Gambrell obtained many needed materials. Richard Gambrell obtained books, made valuable research suggestions, and provided enthusiastic support.

Many of my colleagues at Suffolk County Community College provided information. Tony Di Franco, Michael Gerien, Tony Martone, and Ely Silverman were among those I spoke to.

To say Douglas Rathgeb provided valuable editorial suggestions and served as a sounding board for the basic ideas in the book would be an enormous understatement. His help was vital to the book's completion.

Finally, this book was helped by my mother, Lillian Scheinert Epstein, who transmitted to me her passion for films, and by my wife, Sharon, and children Michael, Elana, and Rachel, whose assistance and support were always available.

LAWRENCE J. EPSTEIN

Suffolk County Community College

Chronology

1882 Samuel Goldwyn born Samuel Goldfisch in Warsaw, Poland, August 27.

1896 Arrives in New York, his name spelled Goldfish by an Immigration official, and is given a factory job in Gloversville, New York.

1902 Becomes United States citizen.

1910 Marries Blanche Lasky, sister of famous vaudevillian Jesse Lasky.

1911 Becomes fascinated by film after seeing two-reel Westerner titled *Broncho Billy's Adventure*.

1912 Arthur S. Friend suggests he go into motion picture business.

1913 Co-founds Jesse L. Lasky Feature Motion Picture Company; *The Squaw Man*, directed by Cecil B. De Mille, is the company's first motion picture (1914).

1916 Helps found Famous Players-Lasky Company (a forerunner of Paramount Pictures) but resigns from company three months later in dispute. Divorces Blanche Lasky. Co-founds Goldwyn Pictures Corporation with the name derived from the first part of his name and the last part of partners named Selwyn brothers.

1918 Changes name legally to Samuel Goldwyn.

1919 Announces formation within Goldwyn Company of Eminent Authors Pictures Inc., allowing well-known authors to become part of the film industry.

1922 Replaced as president of Goldwyn pictures Corporation in dispute. Publishes his ghost-written autobiography, *Behind the Screen*.

1923 Forms independent company without any partners, Goldwyn Productions, Inc., Ltd. *The Eternal City*, his first independent production, is completed; *Potash and Perlmutter*, his second independent production, is his first to be released.

1924   *Cytherea; In Hollywood with Potash and Perlmutter; Tarnish.*

1925   Marries actress Frances Howard Mc Laughlin, April 23. *A Thief in Paradise; His Supreme Moment; The Dark Angel; Stella Dallas.*

1926   *Partners Again* (the last of the Potash and Perlmutter series); *The Winning of Barbara Worth.*

1927   *The Night of Love; The Magic Flame; The Devil Dancer.*

1928   *Two Lovers; The Awakening.*

1929   *The Rescue; Bulldog Drummond; This Is Heaven: Condemned.*

1930   *Raffles; Whoopee!* (the first of his Eddie Cantor films); *The Devil To Pay; One Heavenly Night.*

1931   *Street Scene* (perhaps his first really important film); *Palmy Days; The Unholy Garden; Arrowsmith; Tonight or Never.*

1932   *The Greeks Had a Word for Them; The Kid from Spain; Cynara.*

1933   *The Masquerader; Roman Scandals.*

1934   *Nana* (the first of several failures starring Anna Sten); *We Live Again; Kid Millions.*

1935   *The Wedding Night; The Dark Angel; Barbary Coast; Splendor.*

1936   *Strike Me Pink; These Three; Dodsworth; Come and Get It; Beloved Enemy.*

1937   *Woman Chases Man* (a unique "screwball" picture for him); *Stella Dallas; Dead End; The Hurricane.*

1938   *The Goldwyn Follies; The Adventures of Marco Polo; The Cowboy and the Lady.*

1939   *Wuthering Heights; They Shall Have Music; The Real Glory.*

1940   *Raffles; The Westerner* (one of his few Westerns, starring Gary Cooper).

1941   *The Little Foxes; Ball of Fire.*

1942   *The Pride of the Yankees.*

1943   *They Got Me Covered; The North Star.*

1944   *Up in Arms* (begins association with Danny Kaye); *The Princess and the Pirate.*

1945   *Wonder Man.*

1946   *The Kid from Brooklyn; The Best Years of Our Lives.*

1947   Awarded Irving Thalberg Memorial Award. *The Best Years of Our Lives* wins seven Oscars, including Best Picture of the Year. *The Secret Life of Walter Mitty; The Bishop's Wife.*

1948   *A Song Is Born; Enchantment.*

1949   *Roseanna McCoy; My Foolish Heart.*

1950   *Our Very Own; Edge of Doom.*

1951   *I Want You.*

1952   *Hans Christian Andersen.*

1955   *Guys and Dolls.*

1959   *Porgy and Bess,* after numerous production difficulties, becomes his final production.

1974   Dies in Santa Monica, California, January 31.

1

The Story Begins

MANY OF THE VALUES SAMUEL GOLDWYN expressed in his motion pictures—sympathy for the poor and oppressed and concern for the everyday feelings of common people, for example—were the natural results of Goldwyn's childhood experiences and environment.

Early Life

Goldwyn was born Samuel Goldfisch in Warsaw, Poland, on August 27, 1882. The place and date of his birth are important because the last quarter of the nineteenth century was a time of considerable ferment in Eastern Europe. The general conditions of poverty and political upheaval were compounded for Jews like the Goldfisch family by anti-Semitism and the constrictive conditions under which they were forced to live.

For Jews especially, America was a "Golden Land," and to one young Jewish boy in particular, Samuel Goldwyn, America offered the promise of an escape from poverty and the hopelessness of the life he faced.

After going to work at age eleven as an office boy, Goldwyn sensed the limits imposed on him by others. He decided to leave Poland. As he was leaving an elderly neighbor gave him advice which he remembered throughout his life: "Remember, Samuel, a man's most precious possession is his courage. No matter how black things seem, if you have courage darkness can be overcome."[1]

For Goldwyn that darkness could not be truly overcome until he reached New York, although he interrupted his journey with a stop in Birmingham, England, where he lived with an aunt and uncle.

England might have seemed as bright and promising a land as any for some people, but Goldwyn's rebellious and stubborn character would not allow him to accept it as a substitute for America. After being fired from several jobs and finding himself with increasingly unsolicitous relatives, Goldwyn decided the time was right for him to leave.

Goldwyn arrived at Castle Garden, in New York City, in 1896. The country was greatly in need of immigrant workers so that Goldwyn had barely left the immigration stalls when he was hired to work at a factory in Gloversville, in upstate New York.

His first jobs there were menial, but after befriending the owner's son, Goldwyn advanced quickly and began to consider a life as a glove salesman. In time Goldwyn's innate competitiveness and his ability to bear up under pressure combined with his sure sense of argument to enable him to become one of the most successful glove salesmen in America.

During his life as a salesman Goldwyn fell in love with a woman who eventually married Jesse Lasky, a famous theatrical producer. Despite this marriage, the woman Goldwyn loved, Bessie Ginzberg, remained friends with him and soon arranged for him to meet her husband's sister, Blanche Lasky.

Goldwyn and Blanche met and were married in 1910. Goldwyn's motives for the marriage were questioned by some who felt he was using Blanche as a stepping stone. Jesse Lasky's son believes that "It wasn't much of a love match. Sam married my aunt because he wanted to get into show business and he figured the best way to do that was through my father."[2]

Despite his considerable success as a salesman and his new marriage, Goldwyn was clearly restless. He was still searching. As part of this search he set about to acquire the culture which had been denied to him as a child. He attended the theater and opera, and became widely read. Along with this new culture he became conscious of his appearance, because, to Goldwyn, the outer appearance was the measure of the inner man. This emphasis on being well-dressed, on appearance, later became translated into an aesthetic concern for the physical forms his films would take, how they would appear.

Another dimension of Goldwyn's search was his desire for a job that would bring more status and excitement. The exotic nature of Lasky's vaudeville career was immensely appealing.

An equally exciting possibility was the developing motion picture industry. Goldwyn had been attracted to pictures since an afternoon in 1911 when he saw a two-reel Western titled *Broncho Billy's*

Adventure and was surprised at the huge profit made by so brief a film.

Goldwyn, of course, was not alone in his recognition of the motion picture as a lucrative enterprise. However, for Goldwyn, the idea of making motion pictures was attractive for an additional reason. He very quickly began to see the artistic possibilities, as well as the financial rewards. This new medium, which could manufacture dreams for a public anxious to escape from their everyday lives, was an extension of Goldwyn's own needs. His childhood dreams of escape were reflected in the flickering images in the movie house. He felt an intense attachment to those images for they represented his own dreams.

By 1912 Arthur S. Friend, a lawyer, was suggesting that Goldwyn take seriously the idea of a career making motion pictures. Goldwyn, though, might never have pursued such an idea were it not for a projected change in the import tariff. Prior to the election of 1912, with Woodrow Wilson's victory assured by a split in the Republican party, Goldwyn believed Wilson would lift the high tariff then put on foreign goods. This would mean that foreign glove manufacturers would charge less for gloves than American companies.

Fearing the loss of all he had worked for, Goldwyn began to think more seriously about the movie industry. He discussed such a possibility with Jesse Lasky. As it happened, Lasky had a desperate need for money and was looking for a way out of his own business. Lasky was also personally concerned about his vaudeville collaborator, Cecil B. De Mille. De Mille's adventurous nature was leading him to contemplate fighting in the Mexican Revolution. Lasky believed the excitement of the new picture industry would lure De Mille away from danger.

The Producer

In December, 1913, the Jesse L. Lasky Feature Players Company was founded by Lasky, De Mille, and Goldwyn. Even at this early point, Goldwyn wanted to improve the quality of films being produced. He aimed at making films of five reels (about one hour). There had been no movies longer than two or three reels at all in America until 1912 when Adolph Zukor imported a four-reel French film featuring Sarah Bernhardt. The success of that film led to Zukor's organizing the Famous Players Company, and no doubt served as proof to Goldwyn of the good future for five-reel movies.

There was one additional major problem for the new company—the Trust, a corporate conglomerate which controlled the industry through patents on motion picture cameras and projectors. It was impossible, theoretically, to film or exhibit a picture without the approval of the Trust, and the Trust would not approve of filming any five-reel movies.

Deciding to ignore the Trust, the Lasky Company produced a Western entitled *The Squaw Man* in 1914 (filming actually began in December, 1913). Lasky and De Mille coproduced the film while Goldwyn bore the dual titles of treasurer and general manager of the company.

The Squaw Man made film history. It was the first full-length feature film produced in the United States and the first major film produced in Hollywood. (The original site of the filming was supposed to be Flagstaff, Arizona, but De Mille, in order to keep a safe distance from the Trust, moved the production to a rented barn in the then little-known community of Hollywood, California.)

The film became an immediate box-office success, and this success encouraged the new company to produce a number of other films including *Brewster's Millions, Carmen, The Only Son, The Mastermind, The Warrens of Virginia,* and *The Return of Peter Grimm.*

Additional directors were hired and soon the company proved so sound that its larger competitor, Zukor's Famous Players, suggested a merger. In July, 1916, the Lasky Company merged with Famous Players. The new company was called Famous Players-Lasky Corporation, and, in the new corporate structure, Goldwyn was given the title chairman of the board, acting with Zukor in handling the company's finances. The two men, however, fought constantly. When Zukor threatened to leave the company if Goldwyn stayed, Lasky decided to force Goldwyn's resignation. In September, 1916, Goldwyn accepted $900,000 from the company and left.

Besides being out of a job, Goldwyn also had marital problems. His wife, shy and quiet, was not capable of competing with the famous and glamorous actresses with whom Goldwyn came in daily contact. There were never scandals involving Goldwyn with any actress, but at the very least he was clearly struggling with the moral dilemmas of being married to an unsuitable partner—one to whom he was no longer attracted—and the religious and social constraints against divorce. Later in his life the subjects of marital difficulties, divorce, and adultery would figure prominently in many of his movies. It is probable that the genesis of these subjects lay in these early dilemmas.

Goldwyn would, in a decade (on April 23, 1925), marry again, this time to a beautiful aspiring actress named Frances Howard McLaughlin. Frances was in many ways a perfect wife for him. She organized their social life, she protected and pampered him, and, crucially, she became a surrogate business partner, helping him select stories and talking over with him ideas about those stories. Goldwyn remained married to Frances until his death nearly a half-century later.

But in 1916 no such happiness was available with either marriage or business partners. After leaving Lasky, Goldwyn decided to search for new partners. In December, 1916, he entered into a partnership with four people, two of whom—brothers named Edgar and Arch Selwyn—were Broadway producers. The company was named the Goldwyn Pictures Corporation (from the first syllable of Goldfish and the second syllable of Selwyn). Goldwyn, who did not legally change his name from Goldfish until 1919, liked the new name and began to use it as his own.

The new job was far more to Goldwyn's liking than his previous one. He was in charge of hiring the actors and actresses while performing the usual business tasks required in a film company, such as promoting the film and arranging for distribution.

However, as much as Goldwyn enjoyed his role as president, he was ever-hungry for more complete control and for public recognition.

The new Goldwyn company strove early for quality in all areas of production. Not only did the Goldwyn company hire well-known playwrights such as Bayard Veiller and Avery Hopwood, it also employed well-known artistic designers. According to Richard Griffith the Goldwyn designers, particularly Hugo Ballin, revolutionized the concept of set design. Ballin created sets not just for physical backdrop but to convey the dramatic mood of each scene in the film. Ballin changed the focus from setting as mere background to setting as an integral part of the total pictoral effect. Each shot's emotional effect was captured in part by Ballin's set design.[3]

The Goldwyn company's name became famous for more than just its writers and scenic designers. For example, Goldwyn hired Mary Garden, an opera singer, appearing in the Goldwyn production of *Thais* (1918), and he imported *The Cabinet of Dr. Caligari* (1919). Despite the financial failure of these two pictures, their unquestioned quality gave the company wide respect.

This respect deepened when Goldwyn began to enhance the

quality of his pictures by acquiring good stories. He sensed that it was the story that was the foundation of any good picture, knowing that he, as well as an audience, was enchanted by an intriguing narrative with recognizable characters. What else was a dream?

To create good stories for the screen Goldwyn formed Eminent Authors, Inc. In June, 1919, as a separate part of the Goldwyn Pictures Corporation. He hired Rex Beach, a well-known novelist, to select great writers to come to the studio in Culver City, California, and write for the screen. Eventually selected as Eminent Authors were such famous literary figures as Gertrude Atherton, Mary Roberts Rinehart, Rupert Hughes, Gouverneur Morris, Basil King, and Leroy Scott.

To publicize Eminent Authors, Goldwyn hired Howard Dietz who selected a roaring lion peering through a porthole on which was engraved the Latin inscription *Ars Gratia Artis* ("Art for Art's Sake") as the trademark for the Goldwyn Pictures Corporation.

Although most of the literary writers Goldwyn lured to Hollywood did not find success there, Goldwyn understood better than most producers of the day the causes of such failure. He honestly tried to transform their literary images into cinematic images, a transformation they themselves were unable to make. As Goldwyn wrote in his autobiography:

The great trouble with the usual author is that he approaches the camera with some fixed literary ideal and he cannot compromise with the motion picture viewpoint. He does not realize that a page of Henry James prose, leading through the finest shades of human consciousness, is absolutely lost on the screen, a medium which demands first of all tangible drama, the elementary interaction between person and person (a fist fight on the edge of a cliff) or person and circumstance (a person trapped on a window ledge eighty stories above the ground). This attitude brought many of the writers whom I had assembled into almost immediate conflict with our scenario department, and I was constantly being called upon to hear the tale of woe regarding some title that had been changed or some awfully important situation which had either been left out entirely or else altered in such a way as to ruin the literary conception.[4]

The problem Goldwyn encountered with such writers is best illustrated by his hiring of the famous Belgian poet Maurice Maeterlinck to write a screenplay. After months of work, Maeterlinck handed in a screen adaptation of one of his most famous works. Goldwyn, assuming that he would receive a screenplay befitting a writer of Maeterlinck's stature, was astounded when he discovered that the work, *The Life of the Bee*, had a bee as its hero, and, of course, was totally unfilmable.

Despite his frequent failures, Goldwyn never gave up on literary writers and their stories as the surest source for the best film. Goldwyn's sense of the centrality of story was so strong that even such catastrophes as *The Life of the Bee* could not dissuade him from his efforts.

Meanwhile, Goldwyn's control of the Goldwyn Pictures Corporation was weakened by what some investors called ineffective business tactics; they wanted more money. The campaign against Goldwyn was led by Frank Godsol, who challenged many of Goldwyn's corporate decisions. Finally in March, 1922, Goldwyn was forced out of office as president of his own company.

Out of work again, Goldwyn retreated to Great Neck, Long Island, to consider his situation. He decided first to write his memoirs, but realized that his control over the English language was less than total. He hired a ghost writer named Corinne Lowe, who was a journalist. The product of their collaboration, titled *Behind the Screen*, was almost devoid of autobiographical information. Instead, the book merely highlighted various Hollywood personalities of the day, such as Douglas Fairbanks, Will Rogers, Charlie Chaplin, Mack Sennett, Mary Pickford, and Mabel Normand. Conspicuously absent were any references to Frank Godsol, or other corporate enemies. Nevertheless, there were moments of insight in the book. Indeed, by describing only the filmic component of his life, Goldwyn revealed how central film was to him.

By the time the book appeared Goldwyn had settled with the Goldwyn Pictures Corporation for about one million dollars.

With the settlement behind him, Goldwyn then made a fateful decision: he would produce movies entirely on his own. In that way he would have no one but himself to account to and no one to challenge his decisions. By taking sole responsibility for his films, Goldwyn could then guarantee that there would be no aesthetic compromises in any of his future films. As he once explained to a reporter for the trade paper *Variety:*

I was always an independent, even when I had partners. It's not that I wanted all the profits. But I simply found that it took a world of time to explain my plans to my associates. Now I can save all that time and energy, and put it into making better pictures. Basically I am a lone wolf. I am a rebel. If a picture pleases me, I feel there is a good chance it will please others. But it has to please me first. I don't think I could go through all the disappointments and aggravation connected with making a picture the way I operate if I was not interested in the subject and regarded it as a challenge worth meeting.[5]

Goldwyn formed his new company in 1923, naming it Goldwyn Productions, Inc., Ltd. He was promptly sued by Metro-Goldwyn Corporation to prevent him from using his name (Metro-Goldwyn Corporation had been formed when Goldwyn Pictures Corporation, without Goldwyn, had developed such severe financial troubles that, within two years after Goldwyn's dismissal, it had been forced to merge with Metro Pictures Corporation headed by Marcus Loew and Louis B. Mayer). A compromise was finally reached allowing Goldwyn to use the "Goldwyn" trademark on condition that the name always be preceded by "Samuel." Goldwyn agreed to label the pictures he released with the prefatory announcement: "Samuel Goldwyn Presents."

2

First Films

The Eternal City (1923)

SAMUEL GOLDWYN'S FIRST MOTION PICTURE as an independent producer was *The Eternal City*, made in 1923. (Unfortunately, only a fragment of the original film is extant.) The film, based on Hall Caine's novel, was essentially a remake of a Famous Players-Lasky film made in 1915.

The story, originally a simple tale of love, was altered by Goldwyn to include a political message. The story takes place in the early years of Benito Mussolini's Fascist Italy. Like others of the day, Goldwyn naively believed that the Fascists could bring a new form of democratic government into the world. Goldwyn prepared to portray the central character of the story as a member of the Italian Fascist party. Screenwriter Ouida Bergere wrote the screenplay accordingly.

The plot of the film involves two children, Donna Roma and David Rossi. Rossi had been adopted as a child by Donna's wealthy father. After many years, with the children now grown up, the story resumes just before the outbreak of World War I. Both Donna and Rossi have developed an interest in art, especially sculpture. The heroine's father does not believe that there will be a war. However, war does come. David joins the army and goes off to fight. One day the old man, the adoptive father, receives sad news: a letter reporting that David has been killed. The shock is too much for the man to bear and he dies of a heart attack. Roma enters, sees the letter, and then discovers that her father has died. She, too, is heartbroken.

Meanwhile, the war has caused many problems in the city. Baron Bonelli, a scheming Communist leader who longs to be the dictator, urges his supporters to gain control of the city's fruit supplies. Roma, distressed by the news of David's death, accepts Bonelli's offer to study sculpture in Rome, where, he tells her, she shall become famous. The town gossips begin to whisper scandalous stories about Roma and Bonelli, and begin to call her "the Valonna woman."

David, who had been left for dead on the battlefield, survives the war. He returns to find his house deserted. With his friend Bruno, he begins to search for Roma. As he travels everywhere in search of her, he witnesses so much political ferment and dissatisfaction that he is convinced he should join the Fascist party.

One night in Rome, David, attending a costume party, meets the notorious "Valonna woman." He does not recognize her because of her costume. She tosses coins to David and Bruno after they serenade her, and she, too, is unaware that David is one of the singers.

Roma's most recent sculpture is in memory of David. When David and other soldiers see it carried into "the Valonna woman's" home, they are outraged that a woman of such reputation has created what they viewed as a mockery of fighting men. David and Bruno destroy the sculpture.

Later, David discovers that "the Valonna woman" is, in fact, Roma, but his joy is dashed by the knowledge that she is Bonelli's kept woman. Roma pleads with David to understand and she promises that Bonelli means nothing to her. David, however, cannot forgive her and leaves with the intention of forgetting her. He becomes passionately involved with Fascist politics. This brings him into direct confrontation with Bonelli and his Communist followers. In a dramatic sequence in the film Bruno and David confront Bonelli's thugs in the street and are stripped of their military decorations, and, in the film's dramatic climax, David and Bonelli fight. Bonelli is killed while struggling for a revolver. Roma takes the blame for the murder to prevent David from being prosecuted for the crime. Her actions finally convince David that she had not ever truly betrayed him.

The germ of "the Goldwyn touch" is evident in *The Eternal City*.

Goldwyn was eager to explore new subjects and his choice of Fascist Italy as a backdrop for the love story was innovative and perhaps even daring. By exploring new subjects Goldwyn hoped to find subjects and stories which would allow him to express his own views more fully. Although Goldwyn's choice of Fascism as a model for social improvement seems in retrospect to have been misguided, it nevertheless took some nerve to infuse the already successful love story with political overtones which few American moviegoers of the day understood or, for that matter, even knew about. The film reflects Goldwyn's search for new patterns of social life, where freedom might develop. This search for freedom was developed in more detail in later Goldwyn efforts.

Additionally, *The Eternal City* gave Goldwyn the chance he had been waiting for to test his belief that a producer could be more than a keeper of the company books and a guardian of the corporate purse strings. Goldwyn began to see himself as the key figure in the making of his films.

Starting with *The Eternal City*, and from that point on, he would be the definer of any movie he made. It was Goldwyn's idea that the theater patron should be able to recognize one of his films merely by walking into the theater and seeing the film. It would not be the Goldwyn name on the credits which would define his work as producer, however. Rather it would be the consistent and clearly individualistic style and values revealed in the film itself. This insight was the true beginning and the true meaning of what was later to be called "the Goldwyn touch."

The Eternal City also gave Goldwyn a number of themes which he could expand on in later films. Some of these themes included the misunderstandings between people in love and the feelings of average people who are both confronted with and overwhelmed by events not of their making.

Potash and Perlmutter (1923)

The first of Goldwyn's films to be released to the public was actually the second one he made. The picture, *Potash and Perlmutter* (1923), was a piece of self-mockery based on Montagu Glass's stories and play about two partners in a clothing business on the Lower East Side of New York.

The plot of the film if simple is not simplistic. The two title characters, Abe Potash and Morris Perlmutter, are tailors. They take on a new employee, Boris Andrieff, to work as a fitter. Boris, a Russian immigrant, hastily falls in love with Abe's daughter Irma. Irma, however, is already promised to Henry Feldman, the business's unscrupulous legal counsel.

Boris is arrested and accused of murder after a labor agitator is shot to death. Abe and Morris magnanimously mortgage their business to pay Boris's bail. Concerned that Boris might not get a fair trial, Abe urges him to seek refuge in Canada. Boris is willing to go until he learns that his benefactors have jeopardized their business for his sake. He decides to stay and take his chances. Finally, Boris is vindicated, and, with Feldman's reluctant help, and with Abe's blessings, he wins Irma's hand.

Potash and Perlmutter was so successful both critically and at the box office that Goldwyn eventually followed it with two sequels. The reviewer for the *New York Times* reported that "The picture has as many laughs as a Chaplin comedy."[1] That comedy centered on the frequent fights between the two partners. This, of course, pariodied, not accidentally, Goldwyn's own tempestuous relationships with his business partners, relationships which were well-known and well-publicized not only within the industry, but outside it as well.

In addition, Goldwyn who had always wanted to film these stories, but had not been supported by his former partners, was now able to show that an ethnic comedy thought to be of interest only to those ethnic groups themselves or only appropriate on a Burlesque stage, could, in fact, attract the wider audience needed to make it universally appealing and, so, popular. Indeed, Goldwyn made a fortune from the three films he based on these Jewish characters.

Films with ethnic characters, such as *Potash and Perlmutter*, often contained stereotypes which were a widely recognized part of a theatergoer's experience. Goldwyn did not challenge those stereotypes; he played to them. Although there were many elements of Judaism which Goldwyn saw as positive, such as a concern for social justice, the open expression of passions, and the struggle for freedom, he accepted the notion that the public should be allowed to have its expectations met and so should see the Jew as a caricatured tailor or shifty lawyer rather than a genuinely heroic figure. As a producer of feature films Goldwyn understood that these stereotypes were hardly limited to any one ethnic group, that the barbs did not feed any anti-Semitism, and that, for better or worse, it was the public, not the artist, who determined popular culture in America. Goldwyn wanted to change his audiences, to change their pattern of thinking, but he knew that he would have to acquire a reputation through his films before he could truly have any impact.

Sound Films

After making another dozen films, including the *Potash and Perlmutter* sequels and *Stella Dallas* in 1925 and *The Winning of Barbara Worth* (in which Gary Cooper made his debut) in 1926, Goldwyn, in 1926, Goldwyn, along with the rest of Hollywood, suddenly had a staggering readjustment to make. Al Jolson in *The Jazz Singer* had given the movies a voice.

After the success of *The Jazz Singer* (1927) and the 1928 Warner Brothers release *Lights of New York,* which was billed as the first "all-talking" motion picture, Goldwyn realized that sound had come to stay and that from then on the only successful picture would be a sound picture.

Goldwyn immediately went to work to locate and bring to his studio the best sound engineer he could find. He understood the wide gap between the technologies of silent and sound films. In addition, he understood that his concept of story would now have to dovetail with the new technology. He chose Gordon Sawyer, a UCLA graduate with a degree in engineering. Sawyer turned out to be a master at his craft. Next, Goldwyn asked his screenwriter, Frances Marion, to prepare a screenplay that would fully utilize sound. Goldwyn's ensuing sound feature was *This Is Heaven* (1929), starring the Hungarian actress Vilma Banky.

The plot of the film involves a young Hungarian immigrant named Eva Petrie who comes to live with her uncle, Frank Chase, and his daughter, Mamie. Frank is a subway conductor. Soon after her arrival, Eva gets a job working as a waitress. She meets Jimmy Stackpoole one morning on her way to work. Jimmy, though he is wearing a chauffeur's cap, is really a society playboy. Later in the story Eva is sent to the Stackpoole mansion to work at a charity bazaar. She meets Jimmy again and tries to pass herself off as an exiled Russian princess. He decides to play along and convinces her that he is a chauffeur and that he plans to start his own taxi business some day. Eva offers Jimmy an advance on the money he needs.

Uncle Frank, however, has found Eva's hidden funds and has gambled them away. Eva is now forced to borrow $300 from E. D. Wallace, her cousin Mamie's rich lover. Wallace drives Eva back to her apartment where Jimmy mistakenly interprets their being together as a sign of their permanent relationship. Angered, Jimmy reveals the truth about himself, but when he learns that Eva has sacrificed for him by borrowing the money for his imagined taxi business, he realizes his true love for Eva and proposes marriage. To Eva "this is Heaven."

The film was a stunning disappointment to Goldwyn. The reasons for its failure should have been obvious to him, though. Goldwyn discovered that with sound films even a good technician like Sawyer, a good writer like Hope Loring who wrote the final scenario, and

Goldwyn's own impeccable production standards were not enough.

Vilma Banky was one of a number of silent film stars whose foreign accents made them practically unintelligible in front of a sound camera. On hearing Banky's heavily accented voice audiences roared, and even the most tender scenes evoked laughter where no laughter was intended. Banky's inability or unwillingness to alter her accent led to Goldwyn's decision not to use her in further films despite the fact that her contract forced him to pay her an additional quarter of a million dollars.

Goldwyn did not entirely learn his lesson from the Banky disaster, for in several later films he insisted on starring the Ukranian actress Anna Sten, whose accent was as equally unacceptable to film audiences. Why Goldwyn permitted himself this costly luxury is open to speculation. His own Polish accent was quite pronounced and it is conceivable, if not logical, to think that either his pride in his native language or his embarrassment at speaking with an accent caused him to try to force, in the face of all odds, the acceptance of a foreign-sounding voice on the American public.

Bulldog Drummond (1929)

With the failure of This Is Heaven, and the dismissal of Vilma Banky from further screen appearances, her romantic male counterpart, Ronald Colman, was left without a screen partner. Fearing to cast Colman in another romantic picture, Goldwyn decided to star him in a melodrama. Also, Goldwyn was worried about having Colman face the camera when the microphone was turned on at all. Goldwyn was only too aware of what had happened and what would happen to other silent screen lovers, most especially John Gilbert. Goldwyn was worried despite some obvious differences between Colman and Gilbert. Colman had a manly voice, deep and pleasant. He had been trained as a stage actor and so had experience in using his voice as part of his profession.

Goldwyn wanted to take as few chances as possible while he and the rest of the industry was still experimenting with the technology of sound and assessing the changes and implications of this revolution in filmmaking.

Thus, the decision to star Colman in a melodrama was an action aimed as equally at self-protection as at art. Still, Goldwyn fully intended to make his melodrama as fine a film as could be done.

Goldwyn called on the well-known playwright Sidney Howard to write the film. Howard's job was to make the novel and stage hero Captain Hugh "Bulldog" Drummond, a character created by Herman Cyril McNeile, adaptable to the screen. (The first Drummond book had appeared in 1920 and had been turned into a successful play in 1921. Goldwyn liked to adapt already-proven hits.)

The choice of Howard to do the writing was an important one. Goldwyn had learned well the lesson taught him by Maurice Maeterlinck's *The Life of the Bee*. He still wanted the very best writers, but he knew after that episode that he could only use writers who were willing and able to accept his vision and to tailor their writing not to preconceived literary notions but to the reality of the sound motion picture. Dialogue had become the paramount consideration as Goldwyn assessed the talents of those he chose to write for him.

When Sidney Howard went to work on the Drummond film, he decided to stay as close as he could to the original in the story line. The variations Goldwyn and Howard decided on, however, were important. In Goldwyn's version, Drummond was to become a detective who made fun of himself, a nonexistent type in the films of the late twenties. This gentle self-mockery was, of course, intended to be a satire on the detective and adventure melodramas popular with audiences and whose style was familiar enough to the audience so that the satire could be recognized. As in *Potash and Perlmutter*, Goldwyn mixed a dramatic situation with light comedy. It became quite common in films Goldwyn meant to be primarily entertaining for him to mix genres in this fashion.

Bulldog Drummond represented an important step forward in Goldwyn's gaining control over the entire production. Because of his worries about dialogue, worries that the overly dramatic subtitles used in silent films would sound ludicrous when actually spoken by an actor, he scrutinized each day's "rushes" (all the material that had been filmed) for both the sound quality and the authenticity of dialogue. He continued this practice whenever possible for his entire career.

At this time Goldwyn also began to experiment with a technique first used by D. W. Griffith, one of the founders of American cinema. It had been Griffith's practice to have actors rehearse each scene before the scene was actually filmed. This had allowed Griffith to minimize mistakes during the filming itself. Goldwyn found this technique attractive for another reason. Such rehearsals allowed for changes in the script to be made without necessitating a full run-through of an already filmed sequence and so avoided the tension of rewriting while cameras and cast were waiting. In other Hollywood studios such tensions were commonplace. Dozens of takes of a single scene were often taken before an acceptable version was filmed.

The plot of *Bulldog Drummond* can be summarized briefly. The title character is a former army officer who finds civilian life a bore. He decides to advertise in the *London Times* as a detective and is quickly hired by a young American girl who asks him to get her uncle away from a sadistic doctor who has placed him, against his will, in a sanitarium and is trying to force him to sign away his wealth and property. Drummond plays Holmes to his friend Algy Longworth's Dr. Watson and throws himself enthusiastically into the case. Mixing the business of saving his client's father with the pleasure of wooing the client, Drummond prevails not only over the evil Dr. Larkington, but also over his two cronies Carl Peterson and a treacherous girl woman Irma.

Goldwyn received critical praise and public approval for *Bulldog Drummond*. Colman received an Academy Award nomination for his portrayal of Drummond and William Cameron Menzies was nominated for best art and set decoration. The picture played to packed houses and greatly enhanced Goldwyn's rising reputation.

The *New York Times*'s reviewer noted that the film proved the quality and worth of sound films. "It is the happiest and most enjoyable entertainment of its kind that has so far reached the screen."[2]

The plot of *Bulldog Drummond,* however, was trite and the movie set out to arouse specific emotions in the audience. In this sense it might be claimed that Goldwyn pandered to his audience. This view makes Goldwyn appear as a producer whose aim is popular acceptance rather than artistic achievement. However, it was Goldwyn's intention (an ability he demonstrated in later, more polished films) to combine both popular appeal and artistic merit in a way which had never been attempted before. Part of Goldwyn's development as a producer at this time was to veer toward the artistic.

With that in mind he decided to expand the scope of his material to include subject matter of a more adult nature.

3

Adult Material

Cynara (1932)

GOLDWYN FIRST CONFRONTED THE SUBJECT of adultery in *Street Scene* (1931) and *Arrowsmith* (1931), but in neither film was adultery the central focus. It was in *Cynara* (1932) that Goldwyn finally found the right vehicle to introduce this mature subject as the central element of the story, not merely as a peripheral element. The film presented, in fact, a more realistic portrayal of the motives and feelings of an adulterer than other contemporary films.

Cynara was based on a play by H. M. Harwood and Robert Gore-Brown. When other producers read reviews of the play, they concluded that such subject matter could not be handled discreetly on the screen.

Samuel Goldwyn thought differently. He took *Cynara* as it had been written and translated it to the screen without a major change in either the content or in the meaning of the original play.

The protagonist of *Cynara* is a well-heeled British barrister named Jim Warlock. The film opens with Warlock in Naples on his way to Africa. He is preparing to leave his wife. The story up to that point is then recalled in flashback.

Jim is a respectable and respected married man whose wife, Clemency, trusts in him completely. Clemency decides to go with her sister to Venice, leaving Jim home alone on the very eve of their anniversary. Jim does not mind her absence because Gorla had just ended a romantic relationship, and Jim knows that his wife can be of great help to her sister at such a time.

Because he is left alone, Jim is invited out to dinner by his friend John Tring, a bachelor who is always in search of amorous adventures. At a Soho restaurant, Jim and Tring meet Doris Lea and her friend Millie Miles, who are sitting in the booth next to them. Later

Goldwyn's great discovery, Anna Sten, with Gary Cooper and
Ralph Bellamy in The Wedding Night.

39

that evening the quartet attend a Chaplin film where Doris takes Jim's arm and gives him her name and address.

Believing this to be nothing more than harmless fun, Jim soon dismisses all thoughts of the evening. Tring, however, possessed of a sense of mischief, arranges for Jim and Doris to meet again after Jim agrees to judge a swimming contest in which Doris is one of the entrants.

Once again, Jim takes their meeting lightly, but Doris, who likes Jim, lures him to her home by pretending to have hurt her ankle and to need help getting to her apartment. Once there, she pleads with him to stay with her, despite her knowledge that Jim is a married man. Jim is not able to break free for fear of hurting her feelings and yet he knows that their continued relationship will most certainly affect his reputation and possibly his marriage. He tells her directly: "I'm no good to you. It wouldn't last." Doris, however, will hear none of this. She has fallen in love with him, and her feelings prevent her from understanding his moral dilemma as a hitherto faithful husband. She tells him that her love for him is all that matters.

Despite Jim's best efforts to keep their ensuing liaison secret, gossips soon hear of their relationship and Doris is forced to leave her job.

It is at this very moment that Clemency returns from Venice, still blithely believing that "life would be simply dreadful if you couldn't trust a man." Jim tries to tell her about his affair with Doris but he lacks the courage. He continues to meet Doris secretly; he even gives her money to live on.

Doris, though, is now desperately in love with Jim, so desperately that when he tries to break off their relationship once and for all by sending her a farewell letter, she becomes so despondent that her friend Millie feels compelled to go to Jim's home to plead with him to treat Doris honorably. As Jim and Millie are talking, a policeman arrives to annouce that Doris has poisoned herself and is dead. Jim's letter to her has been found and their relationship is public.

At the inquest Jim is asked to substantiate reports that Doris had sexual relations with other men. He refuses to destroy her reputation by telling what he knows to be the truth, that she did have such relations.

Jim narrowly avoids a verdict of criminal responsibility for his conduct. Seeking escape from the public scorn, Jim and Clemency travel to Naples where, after a failed attempt at reconciliation, they decide to end their marriage.

The flashback sequence ends as Tring approaches Clemency shortly after Jim has boarded his ship for South Africa. He convinces Clemency that her life would be incomplete without Jim and he succeds in reuniting the couple on the deck of the ship.

In *Cynara* Goldwyn wanted to show the real human damage caused by adultery. Tring is his touchstone for the image of the amoral male, concerned for nothing but the satisfaction derived from carnal pleasure and the thrill of the chase. Neither his prominent role in the film nor the characterization of Jim as a "perfect husband" is accidental.

Goldwyn no doubt demanded of his screen writers that the audience view a genuinely good man with honorable intentions trapped by a relationship he neither sought nor wanted, yet was inextricably bound up in. Jim is Goldwyn's "Everyman" in that he is the last person one would expect to cheat on his wife. That his seduction is so easily accomplished, and the resulting damage so severe, points to the seriousness which Goldwyn attributed to marital infidelity.

Goldwyn's depiction of the wife in the story fits his conception of adultery as tragedy. It is not simply socially unacceptable—it can destroy lives. Through no fault of her own Clemency is suddenly robbed of her husband's love, the security of her home, and her feelings of having a secure place in the world. For all Jim's suffering, it is really Clemency who is hurt more by his amorous misadventure. That she finally forgives Jim is significant because, to Goldwyn, the breaking up of the home was too catastrophic an event for him to accept as the film's conclusion, with its implied acceptance of adultery in American life. Such an ending and such an acceptance would have been contrary to all that Goldwyn believed at this point in the evolution of his thinking on the matter.

The Wedding Night (1935)

The theme of infidelity was further explored in the 1935 motion picture *The Wedding Night*. Goldwyn went to his good friend Edwin Knopf to help him find an appropriate property for his discovery, the Ukranian actress Anna Sten who, after the failure of her first picture *Nana* (1934), and audience indifference to her second picture *We Live Again* (1934), had yet to live up to Goldwyn's expectations. Goldwyn had previously cast her as a glamour girl but now hoped to find a more suitable role for her talents.

Knopf wrote a moving story, later adapted by Edith Fitzgerald for the screen, about a writer named Tony Barrett.

In the story, Tony's publisher has turned down his new book. This has put Tony in an economic bind and he is forced to move with his wife, Dora, to a family farm in Connecticut. Dora is pretty and charming but it is clear that she has a preference for the city and so reacts to her new rustic home with something less than enthusiasm. Despite her feelings her love for her husband compels her to stay by his side. She thinks that perhaps if she tries hard enough she can come to appreciate the country life.

Walking one day near his new home, Tony observes some local Polish farmers raising tobacco. He meets Manya Novak who makes an offer to buy Tony's land. Manya's simple, old-fashioned ways and her natural charm appeal to Tony. Manya is worlds apart from his wife's urbanity and sophistication. Tony and Manya begin talking and he is so enchanted by the simple mores and customs of her people that he decides to write a book about them.

He is first attracted to Manya as a character to be studied for his book and then later as a woman. He learns that Manya is betrothed to Frederick although she does not love him. Their betrothal has been arranged, as was the custom, by Manya's father.

Meanwhile, Dora is finding the country life more and more unbearable. At Tony's insistence she returns to New York for a time.

Tony continues to see Manya each day when she delivers milk to his house. Once, when he makes a pass at her, she slaps him. Still, she continues to come to his house, to take care of it in his wife's absence. Tony finds her more and more irresistible as she often stays at his house to hear him read from his work in progress.

Around Thanksgiving a snowstorm develops as Manya cleans Tony's house. Because of the severity of the weather she is unable to return home and is forced to stay the night. Her father, alarmed that she has not returned home, unsuccessfully ventures out into the storm to bring her back. Frederick, in a jealous rage, announces to her father that he is through with her.

Though they are strongly drawn to each other, Manya and Tony keep apart. Manya is trapped between her desire for Tony and her puritanical upbringing. Tony kisses her, realizes her moral predicament, and goes to sleep in another room. Manya's father arrives the next morning and orders her to marry Frederick. She flatly refuses, and her father slaps her, because of her disobedience. The slap only makes her more determined to fight and defy him.

Manya seems prepared to carry out her rebellion, but Tony's wife returns. Sensing that her husband is being lured away by Manya, Dora confronts her challenger and tells her: "With you he's got nothing more than he had with me before it wore off. But what he and I have now after these five years is . . . well, after all, five years." Manya accepts the argument and reluctantly agrees to the marriage her father has planned for her. Dora then tries to convince Tony that they should stay together, but he thinks their marriage is through. He tells his wife that he loves Manya, that she has breathed new life into him, and that he therefore wants a divorce. Dora angrily refuses.

Manya and Frederick's wedding night finally arrives, but after the ceremony Manya rebuffs her husband, refusing even to kiss him. They argue about Tony, and Frederick decides once and for all to fight his rival.

As he leaves their bedchamber Manya runs after him intending to warn Tony. Frederick and Tony confront each other on a stairway in the house and while they are fighting Manya, who has been watching the incident with horror, slips on the landing and falls down the flight of stairs. As she is dying Tony tells her that he loves her. She reaches out to kiss him and dies. After her death Tony sees her image in a vision and waves a final good-bye.

The Wedding Night received high marks from critics for its honesty and intelligence, but Goldwyn still felt hemmed in by the conventionality of his materials and the inability of his film to explore fully the reasons behind Tony's infidelity. Such reasons are not, in fact, adequately explained. Tony's wife is decent and kind. She is loyal and devoted to her husband. There is no hint of marital discord prior to his meeting Manya.

Goldwyn also noticed the other failure in the film: the conflict of the American literary culture and the Polish family farming culture is never fully realized in the picture. Neither is the conflict between these two cultures and the culture of the New England Yankee ever developed.

Artistically, of course, Goldwyn was at the same dead end he had reached in *Cynara*. Once again he had tried to deal with a love triangle, and once again he had stopped short of examining the underlying sexual conflicts which were at the heart of the matter. The very nature of Manya's death points to Goldwyn's unwillingness to deal plausibly with the consequences of Tony's moral crisis. Manya's death is a convenient finale for the film, but not an acceptable resolution of the dilemma. By placing his characters in an untenable situation, Goldwyn had no choice but to resort to a melodramatic denouement rather than face the further consequences the triangle would bring after Manya was married to Frederick. For Goldwyn to have truly confronted the subject of adultery he might well have started his film where this film ends.

It is perhaps understandable that Goldwyn himself was aware of the film's shortcomings, and why they remained. He was not yet prepared to challenge the audience's sense of taste and decorum beyond the point he had already passed. As a producer Goldwyn could not afford to drive his audiences from the theater by offering them material so controversial that they would reject it out of hand. He may have been content, in the area of adult material, just to break new ground.

These Three (1936)

In 1936 no theme was more anathema to movie audiences than lesbianism. The Hays Office, the industry's own strict censoring board headed by Will B. Hays, forbade even the mention of, or oblique references to, what was considered the most shocking example of sexual deviance.

When Goldwyn first became interested in obtaining the screen rights to Lillian Hellman's controversial play *The Children's Hour*, the Hays Office considered the material so unthinkable for the screen that it refused to allow him even to use the original title. It was thought that there was so much notoriety attached to Miss Hellman's play that even if its content was totally altered or even removed, the moviegoing public would still associate lesbianism with any film bearing that title.

Goldwyn could not even make public his acquisition of the property. His purchase of *The Children's Hour* cost him $50,000, and most Hollywood moguls and insiders doubted he would ever get a penny of it back in box office receipts. Still, Goldwyn himself believed that he could make a successful and tasteful adaptation of this sensitive play without alienating his audience. In fact, the very description of the property as a "dead horse" and the accompanying ridicule directed at him undoubtedly spurred Goldwyn on to prove that his critics were wrong.

However, there was no getting around the dictum of the Hays Office. Lesbianism was not a proper subject for the screen and so no film, no matter how discreetly it might portray the relationship, would be acceptable. Goldwyn thus decided to shift the emphasis of the film from a lesbian relationship to the effect vicious gossip has on two heterosexual women. To circumvent the Hays Office's ban on the use of the original title, Goldwyn called his adaptation *These Three*.

These Three is the story of how two young women school teachers, Martha and Karen, fall victim to evil rumors spread by one of their malcontented students, Mary. The rumor is that one of the women has a sexual relationship with her boyfriend. In fact, both women are in love with a young doctor named Joe.

As the lie about them spreads, the women are subject to all the hateful and sly innuendos of the people living in the story's proper New England locale. The rumors take on extra virulence when one of the women is accused of having a love affair with the doctor after he is seen leaving her room late one evening.

Despite the fact that there are people at the school and in the town who know that the rumors about the women and their relationship with the doctor are lies, the accusations have taken on a life and force of their own eventually leading to tragedy.

The key element in Goldwyn's successful transition of *The Chidren's Hour* into *These Three* was Goldwyn's simple transformation of emphasis away from a direct confrontation with lesbianism to the less offensive theme of the destructiveness of malicious rumors. With Lillian Hellman's help, Goldwyn came to realize that the lesbian theme could be sublimated, allowing the real intent to the play to come to the fore. In fact, Hellman had never intended *The Children's Hour* to be a study of lesbianism. She had merely used the subject as a vehicle for showing how narrow minds and petty hatefulness could foster lies about people, lies so destructive as to drive those people to acts of desperation and to damage permanently their sense of self-respect and deny them their rightful place in society.

In *These Three* Goldwyn, once again, seems to deal only obliquely with controversy. As in *Cynara* and *The Wedding Night*, the producer fell far short of his full potential for dealing with a serious adult theme. It might even be inferred that Goldwyn lacked the courage to finish what he had set out to do. This, however, is not a fair evaluation. The very fact that Goldwyn could bring to the screen any treatment of such powerful material is adequate evidence of his courage and determination.

The film's acceptance by both critics and public is ample evidence of Goldwyn's artistic ability. Goldwyn was fully aware that when his picture arrived at the Hays Office for viewing, the Board would, in fact, find references to lesbianism or at the very least to "unnatural relationships." It would be fully within the power of the board to refuse Goldwyn the right of distribution for breaking the Hollywood Code and, undoubtedly, the Board would have so acted had not the film been so tastefully and skillfully produced.

Richard Watts of the *Herald-Tribune* gave perhaps the most typical reaction, finding the picture "a stirring, mature and powerful motion picture that is in every way worthy of its celebrated original, and perhaps, in one or two ways, surpasses it."[1]

4

A Passion for Freedom

Street Scene (1931)

DESPITE GOLDWYN'S EARLY FLIRTATION in *The Eternal City* with the sort of democracy promised by Fascism as a means of bettering the human condition, his later films show a marked preference for dealing with the real needs of real people.

Goldwyn believed that audiences would feel a closer bond with screen characters whose lives reflected their own. Each person's life was important in Goldwyn's eyes. The most common everyday problems and pitfalls of life were, then, also the surest sources for dramatic material.

Goldwyn's memories from his childhood included, no doubt, many scenes of despair, love, hate, greed, and all the other basic emotions faced by everyday people in everyday life. Within these lives Goldwyn saw pressures which forced these simple folk into highly dramatic confrontations with their own beliefs and values. He correctly concluded that there was no better source for the plots of his films than these ordinary experiences.

However, Goldwyn was also quick to realize that his audiences would not accept the mirror image of their own lives. Rather, they wanted to see characters whose problems made their own seem mild in comparison. While still being able to identify with the characters in Goldwyn pictures the audience would then feel safely aloof from the manner and degree of suffering which they saw on the screen.

Some might argue that Goldwyn's pictures were little more than well-produced soap operas, or to use a derogative term of his the day, "women's pictures." Neither term is entirely fair. These labels do not reflect the honest concern Goldwyn had for human beings and the human condition. Goldwyn saw in every person the desire to be more than a cog in society's machine, to rise above even the

Goldwyn's views of life among the lowly: (top) the American Street Scene (1931) [Courtesy: Museum of Modern Art/Film Stills Library]; (bottom) Russian peasants in The North Star *(1943).*

humblest station in life, and to find freedom to be whatever one wanted to be.

Freedom from poverty and freedom from political oppression were the cornerstone of Goldwyn's analysis of human needs. These subjects recur in dozens of his films and form the basis of his humanist philosophy.

Three of the most characteristic of these films were *Street Scene*, (1931), *Dead End* (1937), and *The North Star* (1943).

Street Scene had won its laurels in 1929 as a Pulitzer Prize-winning play written by Elmer Rice. When Goldwyn was considering it for production in 1931, he was warned not to film the play because it was too depressing. Set in a lower-class New York neighborhood, the play centered on the struggles of everyday people to contend with their hostile environment.

Goldwyn characteristically ignored the warnings about such a play and went ahead with the project. He hired Rice to transform the drama into a screenplay. King Vidor was given director's chores and Sylvia Sidney was chosen to lead a top-flight cast.

Both the play and the movie are set in one basic place: the steps of a brownstone which has deteriorated into a slum tenement. The characters meet on the steps, and their conversations reveal just how suffocated their lives are by their repressive and brutal environment.

The central characters in the film are the members of the Maurrant family. Mrs. Anna Maurrant, fearing the loss of her youth, enters into an adulterous relationship with Steve Sankey, a bill collector for a milk company. Mr. Maurrant, suspecting his wife's indiscretions, and obsessively jealous, spends most of his time trying to catch her. Their daughter Rose wants to be an actress. She is tempted by a married man who offers her a part in a stage production in return for her affection.

Another tenant is Samuel Kaplan. Sam has one more year to go before finishing college. His unmarried sister, who works as a teacher, his Communist father, and his mother all want him to go to law school. He is drawn to books, but is even more strongly drawn to Rose. Although Jewish, Sam has never been in a synagogue because of his father's atheism. He tells his family that he does not believe the Jews are better than anyone else; he feels no sense of betrayal in his love for the non-Jewish Rose.

The other inhabitants of the tenement are stereotypes of characters in an ethnically mixed society.

Mrs. Simpson is an unmarried and uncaring social worker. Victor Jones, uncouth and aggressive, desires a relationship with Rose. A prostitute lives in the building as does a young couple having a baby and a loving woman who cannot bear children.

After leisurely cataloging each of the sad stories of the building's varied inhabitants, the film settles down and narrows its focus on the dramatic confrontation between Frank Maurrant, his wife, and her lover.

As a new day begins outside the building, the tragic drama is being played out behind drawn window shades. Sam Kaplan sees Sankey sneak into the Maurrant's flat. He sees the figure of Frank Maurrant moving, like a shadow, toward the doorway. Screams fill the air. A shot rings out. The neighbors, alerted, see Sankey in the window as the shade springs up. A second shot is heard and, as the neighborhood's inhabitants gather outside in the street, Frank Maurrant races out of the building with the murder gun in his hand. The street is seized by panic. The gossip mongers spread their news—two murders.

As the bodies are removed, Sam's sister Shirley tries to comfort the grieving Rose. At this moment Frank reappears escorted by two policemen. He has come back to say a final good-bye to his daughter and to tell her that he did not mean to hurt anyone. As the street fills with curious onlookers, reporters, and photographers, Rose and her brother Willie decide to flee the neighborhood forever. Sam offers to go with them but Rose cannot accept his offer. She takes a last look at the world she must leave behind her and goes to seek a new life with its promise of new hope.

As a film *Street Scene* was only partially successful. Its main flaw, according to numerous critics of the day, was that the setting was too static. The film makes use of the techniques of live theater more than it does the techniques of cinema. The camera rarely moves; it does not dare to become part of the drama; rather, it maintains both a physical and an aesthetic distance. The effect of this on the audience is to view the tragedy from a polite distance.

Instead of empathizing with the plight of the film's characters, the audience is merely sympathetic. The camera's look-but-don't-touch technique was perhaps an outgrowth of Goldwyn's own reluctance to reveal a world truly as sordid as the one he found in *Street Scene*.

The critics also complained that the acting style was far more theatrical than was necessary. Many of the actors did, indeed, speak their lines as if they were trying to reach the third balcony, while others garbled and seemed to hurry their lines. Consequently, many critics found the stage play superior to the film at almost any point of comparison. In his *New York Times* review Mordaunt Hall wrote: "Those who have not seen the play undoubtedly will be satisfied with this screen interpretation. . . . But those who did see the stage production will assuredly make comparisons between the performances of the film players and those who appeared before the footlights, and the verdict will be in favor of the latter."

Goldwyn recognized the problems and shortcomings of *Street Scene* and hoped he would not repeat the mistakes when he filmed a similar story called *Dead End*.

Dead End (1937)

In the year *Dead End* was produced there was a lot of industry pressure for producers to make gangster films. In previous years, especially at Warner Brothers, a great number of successful gangster films had proved the viability of the genre. Such films as *The Petrified Forest, The Public Enemy,* and *Little Caesar* broke new ground in the industry by showing audiences the seamier side of American life. The actors who starred in these films, such as Edward G. Robinson, James Cagney, and George Raft, had become box-office idols.

Goldwyn had refrained from producing gangster pictures because he felt that they pandered to the baser instincts in the audience. In contrast, he wanted his films to be entertaining, to be sure, and certainly to be successful, but for Goldwyn indiscriminate violence and death without meaning cheapened the value of human life. Before Goldwyn would agree to make a picture of the gangster genre he would have to find a vehicle which could transcend the morally indefensible world of the gangster.

With this concept in mind it is easy to see why Goldwyn was attracted to Sidney Kingsley's 1935 play *Dead End*. Goldwyn had seen the Broadway production at the Belasco Theater shortly after the play opened. William Wyler, at work on *Dodsworth* (1936) at the time, was in New York and Goldwyn invited him to see the play. Both men were sufficiently intrigued by the performance to contact the playwright's agent next day and purchase the film rights. Wyler, naturally, was made director of the film.

With his director set, Goldwyn went about trying to assemble the remainder of his production team. He used two established feature players he already had under contract, Joel McCrea and Sylvia Sidney, for important parts. For the key role of Baby Face Martin, the tough gangster in the film, Goldwyn chose the rising Humphrey

Bogart. Goldwyn had seen the young actor in *The Petrified Forest* and was impressed with his portrayal of gangster Duke Mantee in that film. Bogart seemed perfect for the role of Baby Face Martin. For the young street kids in the cast Goldwyn stuck with the "Dead End kids" who had established their parts on Broadway. Leo Gorcey, Huntz Hall, Bobby Jordan, and Billy Halop were appearing in crucial roles in their first movie, but their stage performances were so impressive, and they worked so well together, that Goldwyn was willing to gamble on them.

As director, Wyler wished to film the story on the very streets on which the play was set. Goldwyn balked at the idea for several reasons. His first concern was that Wyler, who was as contentious as he was gifted, might assume control of production and remove it from Goldwyn's own control. In Hollywood Goldwyn could view each day's rushes, visit the set, and, in general, exercise his artistic fiat over acting, photography, costumes, makeup, and set design. If the production took place in New York, his control would be severely limited. Of course Goldwyn's objections had partially evolved from his experiences with *The Eternal City*. That picture had been shot almost entirely on location in Italy, leaving Goldwyn far removed from the actual shooting and hence from actual control. He had changed enough so that he did not want that kind of situation to occur again. Over the years he had grown comfortable with the sort of control he now exercised over his films.

The second concern Goldwyn had involved production costs. To shoot a film on location was far more expensive than creating the picture in a Hollywood studio or back lot. Goldwyn understood, however, that by shooting in the back lot he would be sacrificing the authenticity provided by the actual locale. To compensate for this shortcoming, Goldwyn sets became meticulous and accurate to the last detail. His settings for *Dead End*, designed by Richard Day, were, in fact, so grittily dirty that even Goldwyn himself could not tolerate the realism. As Goldwyn's biographer Arthur Marx related the incident:

According to Wyler, Sam was continually dropping in on the tenement-street set, surveying the filth as if it were repugnant to his sense of aesthetics, and shouting in his high-pitched voice, "Why is everything so dirty here?"

"Because it's supposed to be a slum area, Sam."

"Well, this slum cost a lot of money. It should look better than an ordinary slum."[2]

In fact, Goldwyn spent $300,000 on that set which juxtaposed a posh neighborhood with its adjacent slum. The entire film was to take place on this one set to emphasize the claustrophobic environment in which the characters were trapped. For Goldwyn, however, the painful memories of his own youth in the squalid conditions of his home town would not permit him to be as graphically realistic now. Because of this reluctance to face the truly squalid and depressing life revealed in the Kingsley play, Goldwyn seemed to deal with the content from a distance, to present the backdrop as physical setting only—not as the cruel environment and breeding ground for crime which was the real emphasis in the play. The reviewer for *Variety* accurately pinpointed this shortcoming:

What Goldwyn hasn't done is to enhance the message of the play by letting loose the power of the screen as a form of art expression different from the drama. The Kingsley theme is that tenements breed gangsters and no one does anything about it. The vicious cycle continues with each succeeding crop of children, thwarted in their growth of any sense of social responsibil-

Confrontation of rich and poor: Richard Day's set for Dead End. *(Courtesy: Museum of Modern Art/Film Stills Archive and Michael Anderegg)*

ity by the pressure of vicious environment. The play whammed the idea across the footlights; the picture says and does everything the play said and did, and stops right there. There is no inventiveness or imaginative use of the cinema to develop the theme further.[3]

Dead End is the story of Drina Gordon, her brother Tommy, and his friends. They live on a poverty-stricken East 50's block which is adjacent to a street of luxury apartments. The neighborhood is like a trap for its unfortunate inhabitants. The endless cycle of poverty and crime permits no escape. Characteristic of this tragic circumstance is a young man named Dave Connell who had grown up with the dream of becoming an architect. Now, after six years of study, he is drawn back to the old neighborhood. His dreams have not been enough for him to break free from the endless cycle. Also returning to the old neighborhood is Baby Face Martin, a gangster and killer who has been away for ten years. Kay Burton is also a resident of the block. She, like Dave, is seeking to escape, but they both come to learn that they are imprisoned there with the rest. The other characters who inhabit this block have names like Dippy, Angel, Spit, and TB. Their names reflect, perhaps, the toughness and cynicism they have developed toward life.

In Dave's absence a new generation has grown up the same way his did. For the first time, as he observes them, he realizes the hopelessness of his own efforts to escape. That inability to escape haunts Baby Face Martin as well. On his return his mother denounces him as an unfit son and his former girl friend Francie has betrayed him by her marriage to another man.

For Drina, life in the neighborhood offers nothing but frustration. She walks a picket line trying to get a wage decent enough to take her and her delinquent brother out of the slums. Dave Connell sees his own dream of rebuilding the slum with his skill as an architect thwarted by the vastness of the task and his own feelings of inadequacy. Baby Face Martin finds only disillusionment when he and his henchman Hunk return via backdoors and dark alleys. It is Martin's fate, in the film's conclusion, to be killed by Dave before the government men can get him.

Goldwyn's treatment of the unfortunate inhabitants of the Dead End reveals a characteristic sympathy and kindness. He recognized that he could not extricate them from their hopelessness, but his presentation of their problems, their frustrations, and their hopes and fears shows his depth of feeling for their plight. For Goldwyn

Dead End was not an attempt to criticize but to illuminate. He hoped that the film would have enough of an impact to induce the government to respond to the needs of people in the "dead ends" all over America.

Perhaps his wish was at least partially granted when the *New York Post* carried an editorial which read, in part: "The best thing that could have been done at the last session of Congress would have been to show the film *Dead End* to the committee which crippled the Wagner Housing Act."[4]

Even if the picture had not been honored with Academy Award nominations, *Dead End* was certainly a film of which Samuel Goldwyn could be proud.

The North Star (1943)

The North Star was Samuel Goldwyn's only serious film made during World War II in which the war itself was the setting.

Lillian Hellman, fast becoming one of Goldwyn's favorite writers, had been inspired to write an original screenplay based on the exploits of Russian partisans and villagers fighting the Nazis during the first years of the war. After visiting the Soviet Union, Hellman discussed her idea about the script with William Wyler, and they discussed it further with Goldwyn. Wyler, always eager to film on location (as in his unsuccessful attempt during *Dead End*), was more successful than he had been previously. Hellman and Wyler were so sure the film would be successful that Goldwyn, aware of Wyler's recent Oscar for *Mrs. Miniver,* agreed on the phone, in principle, not only to a story about the Russians but to filming it inside Russia.

For Goldwyn to make a picture praising the efforts of a Communist nation, a nation which routinely deprived its citizens of the most basic freedoms, he had to overcome his own prejudices against the Communist system and differentiate it from the true bravery of the common people. The common Russian, Goldwyn believed, like the common American, had an innate goodness and a hunger for freedom which existed in all people. Goldwyn could also understand that when one nation is attacked by another and threatened with its very existence, that the political ideology was not the paramount issue. The facts were simple: Nazi armies were attempting to deprive the people of the Soviet Union of their right to their own form of sovereignty.

While Hellman worked to secure Soviet permission to film, Goldwyn assembled his production team. Goldwyn selected Lewis

Milestone (who had made *All Quiet on the Western Front)* as his director for two reasons: Milestone's growing reputation as a quality director and his Russian background. When Milestone read Hellman's script he was disappointed, especially with the sentimentality Hellman expressed for the Russians. Hellman, however, seemed unwilling to change the tone of her writing after a lively story discussion in which she defended her story point by point. Goldwyn decided, however, that Milestone was right in his criticism and suggested the story be changed. Hellman, feeling betrayed, argued so violently that, after that meeting, she never worked for Goldwyn again.

Hellman was replaced as screenwriter by Eddie Chodorov. The script, unfortunately, never really got any better. Goldwyn was certainly not willing to make a film which even remotely seemed to glorify the Communist system he despised, and yet he knew it would be hard for the American public to distinguish between the Russian-as-peasant and the Russian-as-Bolshevik. It was then that Goldwyn decided to film the picture in Hollywood. He was willing to sacrifice a degree of scenic authenticity for a more universal message about the common people's fight against political oppression. Thus, even though the actors' costumes clearly showed Russian peasants and the villages which comprised the film's setting were obviously Russian, Goldwyn had his actors speak their lines without accent. In this way Goldwyn hoped to keep the film's message intact without overburdening it with unwanted Communist overtones.

The plot of *The North Star* is straightforward. In their village, two lovers, Marina and Damien, are in the midst of a feast celebrating a bountiful harvest. The school term is over and Marina and Damien are joined by their friends from school: Claudia, her brother Grisha, and Damien's brother Kolya, who is a pilot. They all decide to take a short trip on foot to the nearby city of Kiev. It is to be the first time any of them have seen a large city. Along the way, they receive a welcome lift from Karp, the leader of a wagon train headed for the city. The students' excitement is high, and their mood is merry.

Suddenly a group of Nazi planes swoop down on the little caravan. Kolya's quick thinking saves their lives, but their little village has been mercilessly destroyed by the enemy planes. Marina's father, Rodion, evacuates the villagers. He and the able-bodied men leave to organize into a guerilla band in the hills. They leave behind the women and children whose job it now becomes to scorch the earth and deny the enemy the use of their crops and the shelter of what remains of their homes.

Led by Kolya, the students race back toward their shattered village, away from the Nazi onslaught. On the way they encounter a shipment of abandoned weapons which has failed to reach its destination at the guerilla stronghold. Kolya tells his companions that they must now see to it that the weapons arrive safely in the hands of the partisans. Turning over leadership of the group to Damien, he leaves to join his fighter squadron. (He will later be killed while crashing his plane, kamikaze-style, into a German field battery.) Damien leads his young band of freedom-fighters into the hills using Karp's wagon to carry the munitions.

Back at the village, Pavel Kurin, the village doctor, is in the process of organizing the burning of the homes and fields. Just as the invading Germans are entering it, the town is set on fire. The Germans immediately begin asking the location of the local partisan forces. Rodion's wife Sophia refuses to reveal where her husband and the men of the village have fled to. She is tortured for this act of defiance.

The doctor of the Nazi hordes, Otto Von Harden, supervises the roundingup of the children and he has them bled for their plasma. One of the children dies. Dr. Kurin escapes to tell Rodion and his guerillas of the Nazi atrocities and urges an immediate attack to revenge the dead child. On his return he confronts Von Harden with the depravity of the Nazi's action. Von Harden explains that he is simply a cog in the wheel of the Nazi war machine. He does not like bleeding children or following the orders of his Nazi masters, but he is only one man. Kurin admonishes him for such spinelessness and tells him that a man who claims that he hates what he is doing yet still does it despite the voice of conscience is, in fact, far worse than the man who performs his work without conscience.

Then, just as the guerilla attack begins, Kurin shoots Von Harden. In the savage struggle to regain their village, Claudia dies and Damien is blinded, but the enemy is driven out and those villagers who remain move toward the front to drive out the aggressor from their homeland.

Goldwyn previewed the film with his staff after the filming had been completed. When the staff's reaction was not encouraging, Goldwyn decided to screen the picture before select audiences prior to its general release, hoping he could alter the film on the basis of the public's suggestions.

Arthur Marx notes that "*The North Star* created quite a lot of interest in its preparation stages and a number of Hollywoodites attended the preview to see if it lived up to its advance publicity. It did not. In fact, the audience was quite indifferent to the plight of the beleaguered Russians and even laughed in a few places. Sam rationalized it as 'nervous laughter' brought on by the tenseness of the war sequences. . . ."[5]

Despite the preview audience's reaction, Goldwyn was convinced that it was going to be the best picture he had ever made. He told his staff that it was a picture every American man, woman, and child should see whether or not the movie made money. Despite the Goldwynism, the point made was that it was important to Goldwyn that Americans see that a threat to Russian freedom was not far removed from a threat to their own.

Because he was convinced of the continuing urgency of the film's message, Goldwyn continued to work on it. He reedited the picture and shortened it to make it more palatable to American audiences. Goldwyn himself said publicly about *The North Star* that "In telling the story of the Russian people we can't help but feel that we are telling the story of a people who think, and act as do Americans. Both are peace loving; both love their lands. The pioneering in Russia, as its vast resources were open to development by the people, resembles closely the development of our own West."[6]

Unfortunately for Goldwyn, neither the public nor the critics were willing to agree with him. The film drew generally mixed criticism, and small audiences. Interpretations of the film were so diverse that the picture's message was called pro-Communist in some quarters and even pro-Nazi in others. Goldwyn himself had to admit that the film did not live up to his expectations.

Some critics, however, found much in the film that deserved praise. Howard Barnes of the *New York Herald-Tribune*, for example, wrote in his review that "It is an eminently sincere and sometimes brilliant account of the Nazi invasion of the USSR. . . . There is brilliant direction and acting in *The North Star*. It has obviously been written from the heart. . . . It is likely to be a challenging slug for our side and the post war world in which we are certain to be involved."[7]

Time magazine's review was so laudatory that it could easily have been written by Goldwyn himself. The reviewer saw the picture as "a cinemilestone for four reasons: (1) the first major attempt by the United States to present Russia's war with the Nazis as a heroic defense by the people of their homes, (2) the first attempt to draw the vast struggle by focusing on the resistance of one village, (3) the most successful attempt to show a sickening German atrocity in credible terms, and (4) the most successful attempt to show the decisive role which Russian guerillas have played in defeating the Germans. . . . No other Hollywood film has done the job quite so well."[8]

That *The North Star* caused such controversy did not entirely displease Goldwyn, although some of the criticism, such as the vicious campaign by the Hearst newspapers, obviously hurt him. He could, however, take a certain pride that the film, as his earlier films, had raised the level of American consciousness about the struggle for freedom not just in the United States but throughout the world.

5

Literary Sources

The Literary Form

VIRTUALLY ALL OF THE FILMS THAT Samuel Goldwyn produced had their origin in some form of literature. He took his material from Broadway plays, short stories, and most of all, novels.

In this connection, one particularly misplaced criticism of Goldwyn was that his inability to create his own original screenplays led him to lean on established forms as a kind of artistic crutch. Many critics have accused him of being not much more than an artistic parasite, earning his kudos by the wholesale acquisition of great stories written by others. They claim that Goldwyn's sole saving grace in this matter was that he was smart enough to choose recognized works of art in his pilferings.

Of his eighty films, the vast majority are adaptations of the works of such notable writers as Sinclair Lewis, Emile Zola, Emily Brontë, Lillian Hellman, James Thurber, Charles Nordhoff and James Norman Hall, Edna Ferber, and Paul Galico.

Goldwyn himself never publicly spoke to these criticisms, but it is possible to speculate as to Goldwyn's rationale. The Samuel Goldwyn who came to America was a boy hungry for the knowledge and cultural advantages denied to him in his native Poland. As a young man he pursued with great energy the task of self-education. He immersed himself in a study of the classics, both as an avenue to knowledge of the world and to his own fulfillment as a human being. No doubt as he read the works of the great masters his imagination took him to places he had never been before and opened up to him worlds of great beauty and high ideals. He retained these images and ideals throughout his life, and it is only natural that he would want to share them with millions of other

The immortal lovers: Laurence Olivier and Merle Oberon as
Heathcliff and Cathy in William Wyler's Wuthering Heights
(1939).

people just like himself after he had been introduced to the world of moviemaking.

His role as producer gave him the power to realize not only his own dreams but to make them come to life for everyone. He wanted to transform the characters he read about into flesh and blood people: the tempestuous soul of Heathcliff in *Wuthering Heights*, the high-minded but tortured Dr. Arrowsmith, the willful and vicious Regina Giddens in *The Little Foxes*.

He wanted audiences to see with their own eyes the exotic locales: the misty moor of England, the gaudy decadence of Nana's Paris, the splendid decay of the American South.

Goldwyn believed he could enlighten, educate, and awe his audiences by letting them see and hear and be immersed in worlds created by the mind of a great writer. He hoped that by popularizing the great classics he could instill in his audiences a consciousness which would widen the scope of their own thoughts and feelings and allow them to grow. This is one of Goldwyn's greatest legacies to his adopted America.

Another misguided interpretation of Goldwyn's penchant for adapting great literature was that it was a way for him to offset his public image as a linguistic buffoon. Goldwyn was for many years the source of laughter, not all of it kind, for much of the Hollywood community, due to intentional and accidental slips of the tongue. So common were Goldwyn's manglings of the language that the term "Goldwynism" was coined specifically to catalog Goldwyn's particular mistakes. Such familiar flubs as "Include me out," "I can tell you in two words: im possible," and "I don't think anybody should write his autobiography until after he's dead" made their way from cocktail party to gossip column and no doubt, in time, dented Goldwyn's considerable ego.

Still, it is hard to believe of a man whose films show such maturity and style that the idea for them came out of some petty desire to reinforce a sagging ego. In fact, those critics who dismiss Goldwyn as a literary parasite and claim that his choice of literary classics was a means to easy film success, seriously underestimate the difficulties involved in transforming a great work of art from the medium of the written word to the medium of sight and sound.

Great books convey great depth of feeling. They convey richness in texture. They contain subtle shades of characterization. They probe deep into the minds and hearts of their characters. The problem Goldwyn faced was how to take a great book and bring it to the screen without taking away from it the very qualities that gave it greatness.

The basic building block of literature is the word. In context with other words images are presented to the mind of the reader. The reader's own imagination allows him to transform the images not only into perceptions and ideas but also to generate within him emotions through which he can react to the subtlest of the author's thought.

The basic building block of the film, however, is the image. The viewer of the film is confronted directly by the image. He has no choice of images. Therefore he must accept the image which is given to him and interpret it within the narrow confines of the accumulation of images which follow. He has a narrow range within which his imagination can come into play, but the fixed image he is presented allows him fewer possibilities for interpretation. Once the image has been placed before him he cannot shut it out and replace it with an image which he prefers or which completes more fully his emotional and intellectual reaction to what he has seen. It follows that any transition from written word to visual image leaves a barren and unproductive void which, of necessity, must leave the viewer either unsatisfied or unsuspectingly cheated from experiencing the full depth and richness presented by the literary work. Goldwyn understood, therefore, that if he were to translate great works of literature from their natural medium to the cinematic form, he would have to maximize the viewer's chances for encountering the most accurate representation of all elements of the novel.

When the fixed image of Heathcliff, for example, was placed before the viewer, would that image be at least an honest reflection of the true image or merely a distortion of it? When Heathcliff spoke, would his expression, his tone of voice, and his gaze reflect the true feelings intended by the author, or would they leave the viewer at best guessing at his true intentions or at worst misreading them? Could the setting of the dreary heath if not equal at least approximate the one fashioned by the viewer's imagaination?

In order to increase the potential for accuracy and authenticity, Goldwyn sought to impose the highest standards for every aspect of the film's production from the working screenplay to the last nail in the set, and the final touch on an actor's costume. Goldwyn was willing to concede that no film would ever match the richness of written expression, but with this limitation in mind, he set out to make those great books come alive on the screen.

Arrowsmith (1931)

When Goldwyn produced *Arrowsmith* in 1931 he did not yet have enough experience to make a successful transition from the written word to the screen image of Sinclair Lewis's famous novel. Although Sinclair Lewis had already won a Nobel Prize, few Hollywood producers were interested in his novels because their central moral concerns were not shared by the moviegoing public and because all of his books, *Arrowsmith* included, were episodic in structure. In the novels numerous episodes are used to flesh out and embellish the author's central concern with more generalized statements about American society. In a film, however, an episodic approach diffuses the central story. Unless a film is double or triple the normal running time it cannot hope to encompass all the episodes of such a book. The filmic problem, then, in translating such a literary classic was not only one of transforming the written word into visual images but also of paring down the book to its essential elements. Such a task would become more difficult as the number of episodes in the book increased.

Despite these difficulties, the playwright Sidney Howard was sure that Lewis's important novel could be filmed—and he convinced Goldwyn to try to film it. Goldwyn worked with Howard in considering the necessary deletions and produced a characteristic result.

Goldwyn instinctively knew that the central core of the book contained a compelling story. He concentrated on capturing that aspect while at the same time making a conscious effort not to allow the script in its truncated form to lapse into melodrama. (Goldwyn later used a different approach to this problem when filming Emily Brontë's *Wuthering Heights*. In that movie he filmed only part of the book, but in rich detail.)

The plot of *Arrowsmith* involves Dr. Martin Arrowsmith, who, early in the film, meets and falls in love with Leora. A dinner invitation is rapidly followed by courtship and marriage. The newlyweds move to a small town in the Midwest. Despite the hardship of being the only doctor in the town, Martin does well and is devoted to the welfare of his patients. He becomes involved in the lives of each of his patients and is genuinely concerned with the problems they face.

When a mysterious illness begins to strike down local herds of cattle, Martin uses his medical knowledge struggling to find a serum to save them. His efforts are ridiculed by a resentful state veternarian. Martin knows the serum is successful, and when the state veternarian refuses to help him, Martin forwards the serum to Washington, D.C., and is vindicated. Throughout all his difficulties Leora remains the perfect wife: unselfish in her devotion to him.

Flushed with his new success Martin moves to New York to engage in intensive laboratory work. Buoyed by his own rising reputation, he begins to think of himself as more than a simple country doctor. His marriage begins to suffer when his endless hours in the laboratory remove him further and further from a concern for individual people, including Leora.

All Martin's efforts seem to reach fruition when he makes what he thinks to be an important medical breakthrough, only to find that another scientist has already published his findings after reaching the same conclusion. Martin is dismayed by his failure and leaves New York for the West Indies to fight bubonic plague.

Leora dutifully accompanies him. While fighting the epidemic Martin leaves his wife on an island where he thinks she will be safe from the contagion. Alone, Leora inadvertently begins to smoke a cigarette which has been tainted with plague virus, and dies. After Leora's death Martin realizes his mistaken direction and abandons his status as a great scientist to return to a simple country practice where, once again, he can devote himself to the needs of everyday people.

In the novel *Arrowsmith* the character of Martin Arrowsmith is central to an understanding of the novel's message—that the real goal of medicine is the alleviation of suffering, not the accumulation of knowledge for discovery's sake. Arrowsmith's motivations must be understood clearly by the audience before this idea can be fulfilled.

Unfortunately, Goldwyn's inexperience at this juncture was such that he did not have a firm grasp on the character of Martin Arrowsmith, and Ronald Colman, therefore, could not portray the character with assurance.

Many of the criticisms leveled at the film upon its opening were directed at the disabilities of Ronald Colman's acting. *Variety's* critic said that it was "hard to believe Colman in the title role. . . . [He] lacks the depth to portray such a part or has been permitted by his superiors to seem to be in over his head. At no time does he impart the unquenchable thirst for research, the sense of humility or the idolotry for the older scientist which the author wrote into the characterization. . . ."[1] Margaret Marshall, the critic for the *Nation*, remarked that "The character presented by Colman is hardly Martin Arrowsmith. His . . . has neither the unmodulated voice nor the awkward eagerness of the Martin of the book."[2] Still another critic, Richard Watts, thought that Colman was too British for the part, and too romantic-looking for the role of the impassioned scientist. These are not fair criticisms. For Colman could only be as real a representation of Martin Arrowsmith as Howard's screenplay allowed him to be.

Even with these criticisms, many reviewers gave the film high praise. Mordaunt Hall of the *New York Times* wrote: "Samuel Goldwyn, that pioneer picture-producer who has quite often shown a desire to lead the public rather than follow it, is responsible for the intelligent and forceful film version."[3] Hall included *Arrowsmith* on his list of the Ten Best Films of 1931 and *Arrowsmith* was nominated for the Academy Awards' Best Picture of the year. The film was also nominated for the categories of best screen adaptation (Sidney Howard), best art/set decoration (Richard Day), and best cinematography (Ray June).

Nana (1934)

Goldwyn's next attempt to translate a major novel to the screen marked a regression from his modest achievements with *Arrowsmith*. *Nana*, based on Emile Zola's classic of a fallen woman in the decadent Paris of the 1870's became his greatest failure as a producer. While in *Arrowsmith* he had been able to condense the sprawling novel into a sensible, filmable storyline, he seemed bewildered by the complexities he encountered in *Nana*.

To begin with, *Nana* contained content of such an offensive nature that it could never pass the Hays Office, and Goldwyn could not, as he later did in *These Three*, shift the focus and still retain any semblance of the original drama.

Zola saw in Nana the personification of the decadence of an entire culture. Zola's aim was to shock his readers with scenes of unrestrained passion and lust. He hoped to rekindle the spirit of decency and self-restraint by revealing the excesses of Nana's hedonism.

Goldwyn struggled during the writing of the film to overcome the apparently unredeemable, immoral aspects of the Zola novel. Finally, he was compelled to abandon any effort to make the film an accurate representation of Zola's message; instead he searched for other qualities which he might turn into an acceptable and workable cinematic effort. So far from the original was Goldwyn's *Nana*, that the credits of the film read that the film was "Suggested By" the Zola novel rather than "Based Upon" the work.

It is, of course, possible that Goldwyn misread Zola's intentions in writing *Nana*. The author intended his work to be a warning to his countrymen to spurn the excesses of sexual decadence in order to rede and revitalize the French nation. The figure of Nana was a tool for the accomplishment of that goal. Nana herself as an individual tragedy was of less interest to him. To Goldwyn, however, the character of Nana herself seemed reason enough for the making of the picture. Hers, after all, was a story which the average person could understand and sympathize with because her passion was in many ways only an exaggeration or aberration of their own lusts and human failings.

The story told in Goldwyn's *Nana* opens in Paris in 1868. Nana is a scrub girl who is determined not to remain trapped in her low station. "I won't be weak and I won't be poor," she declares, and seems willing to do almost anything to escape a life of poverty and degradation.

A year later she is in the Café of the Seven Trout, where she is seen by a handsome young soldier in Napoleon III's army. That same evening she meets Gaston Greiner, one of the main figures of Parisian stage life. Accompanied by his assistant Bordenave, Greiner seeks to make Nana a star of the theater. She becomes Greiner's mistress, and, because of her beauty and stage popularity, is soon the most sought-after woman in Parisian society. One night at the theater the Grand Duke Alexis, an elderly admirer of beautiful women, sees her performing. She then has an affair with the grand duke.

The next man in Nana's life is George Muffat, the soldier who remembers seeing her one night in the Café of the Seven Trout. George's brother Andre, concerned that Nana's relationship with George is destroying his brother, offers her twenty thousand francs to stop seeing him. She refuses, but Andre, determined to break up the match, arranges for George to be sent to Algeria. George sends letters to Nana, but these are intercepted by Nana's friend Mimi, who believes that Nana's relationship with the soldier is harming her theatrical career. Mimi also tears up Nana's letters to George before they are sent. Andrew himself, however, soon falls under Nana's spell and suddenly falls madly in love. He provides a beautiful apartment for her and hopes to take his brother's place in her life.

Finally the private lives of Nana and her suitors are overwhelmed by the events of history. War breaks out between France and Prussia and both Andre and his returning brother George are expected to fight in defense of France. When George learns that Andre has

Anna Sten and Phillips Holmes as an infatuated couple in Nana.

stolen Nana from him, he prepares to fight his brother for her affection. In a sudden burst of patriotism and self-denial, Nana recognizes that she cannot allow the brothers to destroy each other because of her. Knowing that neither man can give her up, she decides that neither shall have her, and so she commits suicide.

Nana's suicide is reminiscent of Manya's accidental death in *The Wedding Night*. Once again doomed love is resolved by the convenient death of the heroine.

In the Zola novel, Nana also dies, but not by her own hand. She is, instead, consumed by smallpox, a disease which turns her once beautiful body into a grotesque rotting animal. With this startling image of the once beautiful Nana ravaged and hideous, Zola meant to depict graphically the decay of the French social fabric. Goldwyn knew that he could not present such an image to the American moviegoer, yet Nana's behavior called for her to be punished. By having Nana commit suicide for patriotic reasons, Goldwyn so perverted the image of Zola's willful, narcissistic prostitute, that the image was not only unrecognizable to Zola readers, but, even worse, seemed a gross misrepresentation of the author's intended image.

The character of Andre also suffers in transition. In the Zola novel Andre was like a moth drawn to a fatal flame. He knew that evil lurked within the beautiful body that encased Nana, and he tried mightily to control his lust for her by keeping his distance. Nana's spell, however, was too overpowering and he finally succumbed to her charms. In Goldwyn's version, Andre makes the transition from righteous indignation to hopeless infatuation with barely a moment's thought. So arbitrary is his decision that his very credibility as a character comes into question. The audience cannot accept him as real. Even if they could he has been transformed from the moral conscience of France in the book to a protective, jealous brother in the film.

Richard Griffith points to the considerable speculation that the entire *Nana* fiasco could be attributed to Goldwyn's misplaced admiration for the young Ukranian actress Anna Sten. Since Goldwyn could not let her play Nana as Nana, he was obliged to turn her into the same kind of "effete glamour girl" then popular with audiences. Griffith speculates further that "Miss Sten was equipped to play the real Nana not the fabricated one. Her forthright and realistic acting style which had attracted Mr. Goldwyn in the first place proved the barrier of her acceptance by the feminine audience, for which read for all practical purposes—the movie audience."[4]

Anna Sten had begun her film career in a series of Soviet films. Following her success in those, she went to Germany where, among other features, she starred in *Der Morder, Dmitri Karamazove*, taken from Dostoevski's novel *The Brothers Karamazov*.

On a trip to Europe in 1932 Goldwyn saw her play the part of Grushenka in the film and immediately forecast her success in Hollywood. Foreign stars were then in vogue, and certainly Anna Sten's attractive features and screen presence would make her as popular as a Garbo or a Dietrich, Goldwyn thought. He evidently overlooked or thought inconsequential her major flaw: her accent. Hearing her speak a Slavic language with a pleasant Ukranian accent did not produce the same effect as hearing her speak English with that same same accent. Although Goldwyn did not sense it, he would in time reach the same conclusion about Anna Sten that he had earlier reached about Vilma Banky.

When Goldwyn brought Anna Sten to Hollywood he gave her the complete glamour girl buildup, and by the time *Nana* opened at the Radio City Music Hall in February, 1934, she was, in the words of Arthur Marx, "better known to some Americans than Charles

Lindbergh and the Burma Shave sign."[5] As soon as the critics'
reviews were in it was apparent that Goldwyn's *Nana* was destined
to be a major failure critically. The critics were, it turned out, kinder
to Anna Sten than the public would be; the movie was a box-office
disaster.

The *Variety* reviewer claimed that Goldwyn had "brilliantly
launched a new star in a not so brilliant vehicle. . . . Miss Sten has
beauty, glamour, charm, histrionic ability . . . and vivid sex appeal.
That's the difference between just a good leading woman and a
potent gate-getting star."[6] *Time* magazine's critic gave a mild
backhanded slap at her accent but concluded that she was "a
cheery, wise, and personable importation from Russia."[7] Mordaunt
Hall of the *New York Times* seemed to compliment her by
comparing her English delivery with that of Marlene Dietrich and
noted that she performed the role with efficiency and charm.[8] The
Literary Digest noted that she was "worthy of serious attention as a
performer," although better suited perhaps "to the earthy realistic
zestful school rather than that of the wistful dream."[9] Finally,
Richard Watts of the *Herald-Tribune* found her "a splendid example of the strikingly vigrous peasant type that in its lusty beauty
may end by being far superior to the effete Glamour Girl of the
current school of picture-going in dramatic qualities."[10]

It was word of mouth that did in the picture. The Hollywood
community seemed to revel in the failure of *Nana* if only because it
revealed that the Great Goldwyn, too, could make mistakes.

Anna Sten, unfortunately, seems to have been an unintended
casualty of the picture. Whether her thick foreign accent was the
real cause of her demise as a potential Hollywood queen is a matter
of mere speculation. Both Greta Garbo and Marlene Dietrich, two
of the most respected actreseses in Hollywood and the supposed
models for Anna Sten, had accents as guttural, if not more so, than
the Ukranian actress, and Goldwyn was no more mistaken in seeing
her screen potential than those who had recognized the talents of
Dietrich and Garbo. Anna Sten was simply a victim of circumstance.
The market for exotic glamour girls was also limited. Even some of
the later films of Garbo and Dietrich were box-office failures until
they turned to comedies like *Ninotchka* and *Destry Rides Again*.

Nana was more than just a temporary setback for the Goldwyn
reputation. It brought into serious question whether Goldwyn
himself still retained the almost magical ability to turn out quality
pictures.

After *Nana*, Anna Sten made two more films for Goldwyn, who, despite the *Nana* debacle, had refused to give up on her. In each of those two succeeding films (*The Wedding Night* has been discussed in chapter 3), the critics found her appealing, but the viewing public continued to associate her with the failure of *Nana*, and she was never given a real chance to live down that reputation.

The case of Anna Sten also illustrates the only real artistic blind spot that Goldwyn could not remove from his artistic vision. Sten was a fine actress and her failure and part of *Nana's* failure was due to her being miscast. Goldwyn's search for material to fit actors or actresses, instead of reversing the process, could and sometimes did result in such disasters.

We Live Again (1934)

When Goldwyn cast Anna Sten again in his 1934 film *We Live Again,* he no doubt thought he could right the earlier wrong of *Nana* by giving the actress the lead role in a drama set in her native Russia. He chose as a vehicle Leo Tolstoy's novel *Resurrection*.

Tolstoy's themes of sin, suffering, and redemption were familiar and popular ones with which any audience would identify. With Anna Sten now properly placed in a comfortable and appropriate setting, Goldwyn was convinced that, this time, he could make her a star.

Once more he gathered his finest technicians and actors to insure the film's success. Rouben Mamoulian, who had directed both Dietrich and Garbo in his recent work, seemed the logical choice for director of the film. Gregg Toland as cinematographer would be able to use his finest skills to exhibit the star's stunning beauty as no other camera operator could achieve. Screenwriters such as Maxwell Anderson, Leonard Praskins, and Preston Sturges could be counted on to compress the Tolstoy novel into a tight and well-plotted story. Finally, an actor of unquestioned stature like Frederic March would provide the perfect romantic lead.

Since *Resurrection* had already been treated in four earlier films, the plot of *We Live Again* was partially familiar to screen audiences.

The story concerns a debonair and carefree Prince and royalist officer who woos and eventually seduces a pretty, young servant girl who lives with his aunts. Quickly forgetting her, he goes away to rejoin his regiment, and, while he is gone, the servant girl gives birth to an illegitimate child. The child dies while still in infancy. The servant girl leaves for Moscow and becomes a prostitute. Her miserable condition worsens after she is brought to trial for having murdered one of her customers, a crime which she did not commit. By accident, the officer whose child she bore is on the jury. He is just on the verge of solidifying his social position by marrying into one of the wealthiest families in Moscow.

After a clerical error which results in a misreading of the jury's verdict, she is sentenced to serve a term of imprisonment in desolate Siberia. The prince, badly shaken by the experience of seeing her in the dock, makes an effort to get her released. He even goes to her jail cell to plead with her to forgive him for abandoning her.

His pleading is in vain. Ashamed of his own part in her suffering, the prince feels he must find a way to atone for his sin. Accordingly, he willfully strips himself of all his land and possessions. He realizes that not only he but his entire patrician class has been guilty of grievous wrongs to the girl's entire social class. He returns to her again, begging her forgiveness, and goes with her to prison in Siberia.

Unfortunately for Goldwyn and Anna Sten, the audience found the message of the film as remote as the setting. Despite all of Goldwyn's extraordinary buildup for the film, the result was the same as with *Nana*. After her appearance in *The Wedding Night*, Anna Sten made no more films for Goldwyn and she never became the star that the producer had hoped she would.

Dodsworth (1936)

Part of the lesson Goldwyn learned from his 1931 film *Street Scene* was that it is difficult to translate a work of drama to the screen. The major criticism of Goldwyn's film version of the Elmer Rice work was that it appeared too much like a photographed play.

When Goldwyn acquired Sinclair Lewis's *Dodsworth* he hoped to avoid some of his earlier mistakes. Actually *Dodsworth*, first written as a novel, came to Goldwyn's attention when it was already partially in the form of a screenplay. Sidney Howard, one of Goldwyn's favorite writers, had taken the intermediate step in order to avoid yet another pratfall such as occurred during the filming of *Arrowsmith*.

Both books reflected the episodic style of Sinclair Lewis's writing, a style which did not adapt itself well for the screen. *Dodsworth*, in fact, was even more episodic than *Arrowsmith* had been. Howard, however, had sensed that the episodes which made up the bulk of *Dodsworth* had a rhythm to them and a construction amenable to dramatization. Howard fashioned a play of fourteen "master scenes" and the result was remarkably similar to the form of a final screenplay.

When Eddie Chodorov was given the responsibility by Goldwyn to produce such a screenplay, he determined that it would be a mistake to tamper any further with the piece as presented by Howard. The threads which held the fourteen scenes together were so delicate that any further alterations would cause the structural elements to give way. As Arthur Marx put it, the whole screenplay would collapse like a house of cards.[11]

Goldwyn, however, felt it necessary to join the scenario discussions hoping to fine tune the screenplay. His decision to intervene produced an agonizing series of conferences. It took two years of writing and rewriting only to return to the very form which Chodorov had recommended in the beginning. As Goldwyn saw it though, the two years and the substantial sums of money paid out to five different rewrite men had not been wasted. In being dissatisfied with the Chodorov draft, Goldwyn was merely exercising his artistic conscience. To be dissatisfied and not to try seemed worse to him than the two years of additional effort which, as their result, justified the original effort as being the best possible adaptation of the original Lewis work. With all this work Goldwyn no doubt found *Dodsworth* a significant educational experience which would prepare him for later challenges, including the immense amount of work he did on the complex and compelling film *The Best Years of Our Lives*.

With the screenplay problems solved to his grudging satisfaction, Goldwyn then proceeded on a typically Goldwynesque talent hunt. His choice of director was William Wyler, who was to become Goldwyn's collaborator on a series of literary classics. The working relationship of Wyler and Goldwyn was basically an artistic form of the adversary system. Both men were strong-willed and had well-entrenched views of artistic integrity and technical expertise. Both men saw the film as a reflection of their own personal integrity and standards of taste. Though they disagreed more often than not, they were totally in agreement on the question of the screenplay for *Dodsworth*.

Despite Goldwyn's acceptance of Chodorov's fourteen scenes, both Goldwyn and Wyler had the distinct impression that the plot line of the play needed strengthening. They therefore added a number of events previously alluded to but not actually shown, as well as numerous details meant to give the script a higher degree of authenticity.

Authenticity was a problem they also faced in the setting of the picture. Most of the book was set in various European locales. The cost of sending the entire cast and crew to Europe was prohibitive so Wyler and Goldwyn dispatched a camera crew with very detailed instructions to film backgrounds for a series of process shots in the film. (A process shot—also known as rear projection—actually consists of two shots. In the case of *Dodsworth* the series of backgrounds filmed in Europe would be processed in Hollywood and projected on a special screen at the back of the set. The projector was placed behind the screen. While these background images were on the screen the actors were performing before cameras in front of the screen. The appearance of the rear projection and the live actors and actresses being filmed in front of it gave the appearance of the stars standing not in the studio but in the actual location where the original background was filmed.)

Goldwyn's talent search did not stop with Wyler. He proceeded to hire Walter Huston for the title role. Huston had starred in the Broadway version of the novel and was an excellent actor even though he was not a box-office attraction. To complement Huston, the two female leads were played by Ruth Chatterton and Mary Astor. The young David Niven also appeared—in the first of nine appearances in Goldwyn pictures—in the role of Captain Clyde Lockert.

The story in *Dodsworth* begins in Zenith, Ohio. Sam Dodsworth agrees to sell his automobile business and to retire as his wife has insisted. The Dodsworths plan to travel to Europe. Sam, though, accepts the end of his business career grudgingly and complains "I'll enjoy life now if it kills me, and it probably will." He agrees to the trip in deference to his wife who has, for years, yearned for such a broadening experience. She loathes Zenith and its quaint provincialism and looks forward to the cosmopolitan and sophisticated capitals of Europe. Fran Dodsworth is uncomfortable with the realization that she is growing old. She is almost surprised that her daughter is married and expecting a child; she hopes the trip will help her recapture her youth and forget the truth: that she is about to become a grandmother.

Sam is satisfied with the thought that he is going to visit new and exciting places; for Fran there is a need to find new friends. Sam is in search of culture while Fran seeks to experience relationships different from those she had in Zenith.

On board the ocean liner Sam takes leisurely strolls along the deck while Fran begins a flirtation with Captain Clyde Lockert, a dashing young Englishman who seems at first to be attracted to Fran but who reject her when he realizes how naive she is about liaisons.

Once in England Sam is soon caught up in learning about and experiencing British culture. He meets Edith Cortwright, (Mary Astor), a divorcee, who enchants him.

From London the Dodsworths move on to Paris, and while Sam goes sightseeing his wife accompanies a friend to a restaurant where they meet Arnold Iselin. Iselin becomes Fran's escort and together they go to Biarritz. The trip becomes the beginning of their relationship.

Sam, meanwhile, has soaked up as much culture as he can stand and is ready and willing to return to America. Fran tells him flatly that she is not ready to leave, claiming that for her the vacation has just begun. Following an argument on the subject, Fran moves out of the hotel and rents a separate villa for herself.

Sam sails back to America alone. On his arrival, even the comfort of his daughter cannot cheer him. He misses his wife greatly and sends for her to return. Again, she refuses. He decides to return to Paris and bring her back with him. By the time he arrives, Fran has broken with Iselin and has met the poverty-stricken but proud Baron Kurt von Obersdorf. Von Obersdorf falls in love with Fran and wants to marry her. She loves the baron as well.

When Sam confronts his wife in Paris she is unmoved. She tells him again that she will not return. Fran forbids him from mentioning the fact that they have become grandparents. Then she directly informs him that she wishes a divorce so she can marry the impoverished baron. Sam stoically accepts the situation and resumes his travels around Europe.

In Italy he again meets Edith Cortwright. Their meeting leads to a relationship and love. Edith makes Sam feel young again. He even considers coming out of retirement to go into the airline business.

Meanwhile Fran is introduced to the baron's mother who tells Fran that she cannot permit such a marriage because Fran is too old to bear the children Kurt needs for the continuation of the family line. Fran, stunned by the baroness's decision, then calls Sam to beg

Walter Huston and Ruth Chatterton as the disaffected couple in Dodsworth.

his forgiveness. Edith fights for him, declaring: "I won't see you killed by her selfishness."

Sam decides that his place is with his wife, and so he prepares to return with her to their home in Zenith. As their boat readies to sail Sam and Fran try to revive their relationship. Sam observes his wife's behavior during the ship's bon voyage party and suddenly sees in her the same symptoms of restlessness and dissatisfaction which led to her earlier abandonment of him. He senses that it will only be a matter of time before she leaves him again or destroys him. He looks at her and simply says: "Love has got to stop someplace short of suicide." In the final scene of the film, Sam returns to Edith Cortwright, to live with her permanently.

The reviews for *Dodsworth* vindicated Goldwyn's reputation as one of the finest artists making films in Hollywood. Many of the critics' reviews bordered on ecstasy, and it was clear that, once again, Goldwyn's quest for the finest had reaped dividends.

Walter Huston received an incredible amount of praise for his efforts. Frank S. Nugent, for example, wrote that: "Mr. Huston still is foremost, lending a driving energy and a splendid vitality to the character. . . . It must be a studied characterization, but we are never permitted to feel that, for Mr. Huston so snugly fits the part we cannot tell where the garment ends and he begins."[12]

Ruth Chatterton and Mary Astor received similar praise, and the film received Academy Award nominations covering almost every aspect of the film's production.

Dodsworth succeeded because its theme was basic and clearly stated. Goldwyn had taken characters from the highest social level, characters whose daily lives had little in common with the average person, and had made the problems of those people seem real and universal to average American moviegoers. In this way, Goldwyn was saying that there really were no class distinctions when it came to art and that money (or lack of it) did not necessarily create situations of dramatic interest. The fact that Dodsworth is a capitalist and has a social position which would set him apart from, say, the inhabitants of the tenement in *Street Scene,* does not protect him from the complexities of life, including a broken marriage and dissatisfaction with his retirement.

Sam Dodsworth is a truly sympathetic character. He is honest, respectable, has no visible vices, and merely expects to be treated fairly. He believes that he has earned the right to retire with a certain degree of comfort, satisfaction, and security, and the audience can immediately identify with the central element of his personality which defines these characteristics: his goodness.

In this way he is quite similar to both Tony Barrett in *The Wedding Night* and Jim Warlock in *Cynara.* Like these two characters, he is both victimized and redeemed by women. Like Tony and Jim he enters into an adulterous relationship. Although Tony and Jim are lured from their wives by other women (unintentionally, in the case of Manya luring Tony), Sam does not leave his wife until Fran's betrayal of his trust is obvious.

Similarly, Fran resembles both Manya Novak of *The Wedding Night* and Doris Lea of *Cynara* in her character (though not in relationship to the male protagonist). All three women are dissatisfied with life. Fran's desperate search for a chance to relive her youth leads to adulterous relationships and the end to her marriage. Doris Lea has a desperate need for love in an otherwise empty life. Manya hates her betrothed and the life that is inevitable so much that Goldwyn cannot bear to let her live that life.

Edith, in contrast, reflects both the patience and devotion seen in

Clemency Warlock and the honest righteousness seen in Dora Barrett.

This pattern of a decent man tempted by one woman and redeemed by another is also evident in *Nana* where the temptress and the redeemer are one and the same person.

The recurrent pattern leaves open for speculation the possibility that Goldwyn was not merely pilfering haphazardly the great works of literature, or the popular works of his day for that matter, but that he consciously chose works over an extended period of time which reflected themes central to his vision, or moved that vision into sharper focus.

For example, until *Dodsworth*, an adulterous relationship in a Goldwyn film had always ended in nothing less than tragedy and unhappiness. Admittedly, it was not Goldwyn who wrote *Dodsworth* or who conceived the idea of how adultery affects the lives of the people touched by it, but Goldwyn saw in the writings of Sinclair Lewis, and specifically in *Dodsworth*, a further refinement of his own evolving attitude. Of course, it might be said that Goldwyn himself, in his own life, experienced the loss of one woman's love, and a redemption by another woman. Clearly, however, his life exactly translated into the films he made, the subjects of adultery, broken marriages, and renewed relationships were on his mind. It is possible to see the maturing reflections about his own experiences in his succeeding films.

In *Dodsworth*, for example, for the first time in a Goldwyn film, the main character enters into an adulterous relationship and is not punished for it. Since Sam Dodsworth is the victim of his wife's thoughtless infidelities he is given the right to pursue love where he can find it and where it becomes meaningful for him. If he is to be considered an adulterer it is only because in a technical sense he is living with one woman while still married to another.

But *Dodsworth*'s message is clear: there should be no retribution for the victim.

Wuthering Heights (1939)

The story of how *Wuthering Heights* came to be produced is an improbable one. Two popular screen writers, Ben Hecht and Charles MacArthur, were staying at the Vermont home of their friend, critic Alexander Woollcott. What began as clever table chatter evolved first into shop talk and then into a serious discussion about film-making. Somehow the conversation got around to Emily Brontë's classic gothic novel *Wuthering Heights*, which, the writers decided, would be a real test for the skills of any screenwriter. Its plot was enormously complicated, its setting dramatic, its characters remote, even alien from normal people. In any case, Hecht and MacArthur decided it might be fun to try to do the impossible, and they wrote a screenplay of the novel. They thought the screenplay quite good.

Their main goal in the writing had been to pare down the story to its basic romantic elements. They found the core of what they were looking for in the first seventeen chapters of the Brontë book, and so the two screenwriters virtually eliminated the majority of the novel's characters, including an entire second generation. They chose as their center the tragic love story of two couples, Heathcliff and Cathy and Edgar and Isabella. This also enabled them to sidestep the censors from the ubiquitous Hays Office by removing all the "offensive" aspects of the book, most especially the numerous allusions to incest.

Hecht and MacArthur—who had from 1934 to 1936 produced four films of their own, two failures—knew enough about Hollywood reality to realize that selling their idea would be a task equally as difficult as the writing, but they agreed it could be done if they could approach producers with a finished screenplay. The traditional rule, which they were intentionally breaking, was that the book itself, or a treatment of the book, would usually be presented to a producer for his approval. If he liked the idea he would pay them to turn it into a screenplay, and from there it could reach the screen.

Hecht and MacArthur had taken a chance by writing a completed screenplay before a producer had agreed to see it. Their reputations were at stake, for if a screenplay which they thought so highly of was rejected out of hand by the major Hollywood producers they might blacklist themselves right out of the studios. Besides that, Hecht and MacArthur were writing out of their element. Hecht, for example, was known for fast-paced contemporary trifles of dubious artistic merit. His writing was clever and witty but generally lacked depth. For someone like Hecht to work on translating classic literature, a drastic change in writing style was called for. It was Hecht, after all, who was on record as a writer who worked solely for the money. He had bragged that his previous screenplays had sometimes been written in a couple of days.

Hecht's confidence in his *Wuthering Heights* screenplay was not shared by any of the producers to whom he showed the script. Eventually, however, producer Walter Wanger brought the much-

rejected work to Samuel Goldwyn. Goldwyn was aware that the
Hollywood film community considered the script a pariah. There
was extreme reluctance on the part of actors and directors to be
even considered for work on such a project. And even though he
had successfully transformed the seemingly impossible *The Children's Hour* to the screen, Goldwyn, along with all others in
Hollywood, considered *Wuthering Heights* to be absolutely impossible to get on film. Wanger admitted to Goldwyn that he had a
problem and asked Goldwyn for an honest appraisal. More to the
point, he wanted to know if Goldwyn thought that any changes
would make the screenplay suitable for production. Goldwyn's
advice to Wanger must have been bewildering. First he told
Wanger, "It's the best damn script I've read in years. You'd be
crazy to change it." This praise prompted Wanger to ask Goldwyn
to buy it from him. Goldwyn's response was: "I wouldn't think of it.
That Heathcliff is too damn nasty."[13]

Wanger then took the script to William Wyler, who, in turn,
brought it back to Goldwyn hoping to convince him of its merit and
to let Wyler himself direct. Goldwyn's reaction was still negative.
When Wyler reminded Goldwyn that the film had the makings of a
great love story, Goldwyn replied, "I don't like stories with people
dying in the end."[14]

That seemed to end the possibilities of Goldwyn making the
picture. Months passed before Goldwyn was again confronted with
the *Wuthering Heights* problem. Wyler phoned Goldwyn one day
and told him that Jack L. Warner, head of Warner Brothers Studios,
had taken an interest in the script and was planning on casting Bette
Davis in one of the leading roles. In essence Wyler was telling
Goldwyn that this was his last chance.

The entrepreneur in Goldwyn could not resist the chance of
stealing a property from right under the nose of a major competitor.
In this case, where artistic sensitivity could not be called upon to
prevail, Goldwyn's acute business instincts were available. Goldwyn
got his screenplay, but not everyone was convinced that his business
connivings would result in art.

Variety thought the story as difficult to film as Hecht and
MacArthur had originally imagined it to be. The *Variety* correspondent wrote: "*Wuthering Heights* in theme, characters, plot and
setting possesses not one familiar attribute for which studio scenario
departments search zealously through thousands of manuscripts,
plays, novels, and synopses. It violates all the successful rules of

successful film stories. Its leading characters are something less than sympathetic—they are psychopathic exhibits. And the ending is stark, dire, tragic, and uncompromising finale which utterly disregards all popular theories of screen entertainment."[15]

An editorial in the *London Times* expressed the opinion that although "Mr. Goldwyn is a legendary figure who has a fine, autocratic way with the English language and chronology and things like that," there is no assurance "that the film will be even remotely identifiable with the book."[16]

Goldwyn listened to the *Times*. Although he knew better than to tamper with the Hecht-MacArthur screenplay (his experience of working for two years on the fruitless attempt to obtain a better rewrite of his *Dodsworth* script having proved educational) he still could not accept a film which ended in the death of both the hero and the heroine.

With the addition of John Huston as a writer, Goldwyn's rapidly forming production team was taking shape. Goldwyn continued to argue for an ending less depressing, and therefore more palatable, to contemporary audiences, but neither Huston nor Wyler agreed with him.

Willing to let this disagreement slide for the time being, Goldwyn began to consider the other major aspects of the film's production still requiring decisions. It was determined that an all-British cast was necessary for authenticity of character. It was easy enough to find British actors for the secondary parts, and even for most of the leading roles. There remained, however, the problem of casting Heathcliff.

At that time in Hollywood a young British actor was struggling to find appropriate parts. Laurence Olivier was as foreign a name in Hollywood circles as it was native to the playbills of London's Old Vic Theatre Company.

Olivier's lingering inactivity made him a regular hanger-on at the Beverly Hills Tennis Club, where both Wyler and Charles Mac-Arthur played tennis. MacArthur's wife, the actress Helen Hayes, noticed the decidedly unhappy and moody Olivier leaning against a fence at the club. She sensed immediately that there was the Heathcliff Goldwyn had been looking for.

Goldwyn, of course, was not eager to take chances with unknowns. The Goldwyn touch had not come about by accident and it could not have been without some misgivings that he considered altering his already proven formula for success. But to Goldwyn's own surprise, he had the same reaction to the young Olivier as Helen Hayes had had. Goldwyn was convinced that he had found his Heathcliff.

Unfortunately, Olivier had conditions for accepting the role. He would not take the part unless his girlfriend Vivien Leigh played opposite him. Goldwyn balked at this suggestion. The Goldwyn formula could stand the strain of taking a chance on one new talent, but two was out of the question. Olivier, considering the rebuff to be humiliating, packed his bags and returned to London.

By this time, however, William Wyler, too, was convinced that Olivier was the only Heathcliff for the film. Wyler went to London to renegotiate. Unfortunately, he found Olivier even more adamant in his demands than before, and he was forced to conclude that further efforts to sign the temperamental young actor would only prove fruitless.

Olivier, for his part, still had plans to get the part of Catherine for Vivien Leigh even if he could not be Heathcliff. In fact, Wyler was willing to cast her in the role of Isabella, but she insisted that she wanted to be cast only as Cathy. Wyler tried to explain that this was impossible, since he knew that Goldwyn wanted Merle Oberon for that role. After prolonged discussions Olivier finally accepted the role of Heathcliff with Merle Oberon as his co-star, and Vivien Leigh went on to make *Gone With the Wind*.

Goldwyn's troubles were not over yet, however. For after the signing of Olivier, Goldwyn became embroiled in a characteristically animated argument with William Wyler over where to film *Wuthering Heights*. Wyler offered his long-standing position that, for authenticity's sake, the film should be shot on location. Wyler had taken this same position during his work on two previous films for Goldwyn, *Dead End* and *Dodsworth*. For Wyler the use of actual locations was imperative. Goldwyn, who had experienced a distinct uneasiness about his loss of editorial control over the filming of *The Eternal City*, and ever-mindful of the company purse strings, felt such location shooting was a costly luxury which he could do without. Besides, he had faith in his technicians and fully expected the final studio sets and back lots to present as faithful and accurate a setting for *Wuthering Heights* as the original locales themselves.

As in *Dodsworth*, Goldwyn agreed to send a second unit to England to film scenery for rear-screen projections, and he literally transformed a barren area in the San Fernando Valley into a perfect replica of the English countryside, replete with misty moors, craggy stone walls, and real, imported heather. He even had a thousand panes of stained glass especially made to match the window glass common to the period in which the film was set.

His only break from perfect authenticity, in fact, was his change of the historical setting of the book. The book was set in the late eighteenth century; Goldwyn's film moved the setting up to 1841. His major reason for this change was a personal distaste for the dresses of the late 1700s. Goldwyn thought that a plunging neckline was more attractive for his leading lady, Merle Oberon, than the high collar fashions of the actual era.

Goldwyn's quest for authenticity began to border on obsession when he hired an animal trainer to see to it that farmyard livestock would quack, moo, whinny and neigh on cue, and that the animals would not interfere with the dialogue of the actors when the animal sounds were not required. To insure this, Goldwyn considered cutting the vocal chords of ducks and geese, and, although organizations such as the A.S.P.C.A. and bands of animal lovers objected strenuously, Goldwyn's wishes were, as usual, carried out.

There was still mayhem among the actors. Goldwyn had inadvertently assembled a group of actors and crew whose dislike for one another was as deep as it was obvious. David Niven, who had worked briefly in *Dodsworth,* had developed an intense dislike for William Wyler. Similarly, Merle Oberon could not tolerate Oliver for more than short periods, and the two routinely exchanged brickbats in front of the crew. On more than one occasion they had to be cajoled back on to the set after one or the other or both had stormed out.

With such fearsome animosity and contempt for each other, it is astounding that they could even speak lines to each other, much less pretend to make love when the script required it. Goldwyn himself became more and more alarmed by the growing tendency of Olivier to be excessively histrionic. The more Goldwyn saw of Olivier's evolving characterization of Heathcliff the less he liked it. Subtle hints directed at Wyler and demands for reshooting of Olivier's scenes did not alleviate the problem, and Goldwyn felt compelled to take Olivier aside and try to reason with him. Olivier seemed to get the point and altered his acting style to fit the Goldwyn image.

Goldwyn's troubles were still not over: he insisted that an ending which would leave both the hero and the heroine dead was unacceptable. When he again confronted Wyler with his misgivings the director flatly informed him that he did not think there could be a change: the film had reached its logical conclusion, the ending had been filmed, and the hero and heroine were, indeed, dead.

It was then that Goldwyn believed he had come up with a perfect solution. He recalled the ending he had filmed for *The Wedding Night* in which Manya, after her death, reappears to Tony in a vision. Heathcliff and Cathy, Goldwyn informed Wyler, would be reunited in Heaven and Wyler would film it that way. Wyler refused to comply with a request he considered tasteless and inaccurate at best and, at worst, completely ludicrous. Wyler believed that audiences would laugh at the improbability of such a scene, and that critics and Hollywood gossips would use that single lapse of decorum to attack the entire picture.

Goldwyn, however, was convinced. He decided that if Wyler would not film the ending then someone else would. Goldwyn then put Wyler on suspension from his directorial duties.

Although Wyler and Goldwyn's serious falling out over the ending of *Wuthering Heights* is symbolic of their entire working relationship, it was possible for them to compromise divergent opinions when compromise was imperative. For example, when Wyler argued that the physical world of *Wuthering Heights* could only be recreated against a backdrop of real places, Goldwyn insisted on the propriety of using process shots and authentic sets. So strong was each man's view that the production of the picture with Wyler as director might easily have stood still for days or months, or might never even have been completed. William Lyon Phelps has described the nature of the compromise which led to the unique photographic style of *Wuthering Heights:* "*Wuthering Heights* came from a person [Emily Brontë] who lived entirely in her imagination; the persons she created were more real to her than the persons she saw on the street."

Richard Griffith amplifies this view:

The setting for the film was not the moors of Yorkshire but a wilderness of the imagination. To have produced on the screen any large expanse of landscape would have been to chain the story and its characters to the actual. Instead [Gregg] Toland and Wyler devised a close-in camera work which, in every shot, seemed to show only a small part of the whole scene, in which roads, crags, housetops, and human figures were revealed in outline against dense grays or blacks. Thus was created a chiaroscuro country of the mind in which the passionate Brontë figures can come credibly alive. It was a daring experiment, owing something to the example of the once-admired German studio films of the twenties, and like them it might have seemed today to exude a faint odor of plaster and machinery. That the spell holds is due to the fact that cameraman and director were aware of the peril in which they stood; instead of proudly parading their artifice they make all vague, moony, nebulous; each shot is whisked away and replaced by its reverse angle as quickly as the action allows.

Thus the physical world of this *Wuthering Heights* exists only for the moment it is seen."[17]

The fact that Goldwyn and Wyler were able to reach a new consensus is important for two reasons. First and most naturally, it allowed the film to be completed. Second, however, it also allowed both men, by virtue of their combined vision, to arrive at a striking new photographic approach to the Brontë material, an approach resulting in a style and sense of atmosphere that could not have been achieved through either man's previous artistic position. The major credit belongs to Goldwyn because he had the final say and could have simply rejected Wyler's views and replaced him. Instead Goldwyn listened, fought, and realized how his film could be made better.

Wuthering Heights starts out in a snowstorm. Using the flashback technique, the film relates the story as seen through the reminiscences of Ellen Dean, the housekeeper.

Heathcliff, a foundling, a gypsy supposedly, is taken in by the master of Wuthering Heights, Mr. Earnshaw. The old Earnshaw grows to love the untamed Heathcliff more than his own son Hindley. Hindley despises Heathcliff, calling him "Gypsy scum." Hindley's sister Cathy defends Heathcliff, calling him "a prince in disguise."

As they grow up, Cathy and Heathcliff are constant companions. They play on the moors and in a make-believe castle under Peniston Crag.

The death of Mr. Earnshaw brings to an end this happy chapter in their lives, for Hindley, now the master of Wuthering Heights, throws Heathcliff out and demotes him to stable boy; but Cathy's fondness for Heathcliff develops into love as the couple emerges from childhood.

Hindley, meanwhile, has become a drunkard, and has taken to treating everyone, especially Heathcliff, with cruelty. Cathy urges Heathcliff to leave Wuthering Heights because she cannot stand to see the way her brother treats him. But Heathcliff is so much in love with Cathy that he is even willing to accept Hindley's tyranny if only to remain near to her.

One day Cathy is at an elaborate party at the home of the Lintons, wealthy people who live nearby. Heathcliff's attempts to attend the party are rebuffed, for Heathcliff is only a stable boy, and as far as the Lintons are concerned he has no business being where he does not belong. Heathcliff is enraged by this insult and runs away promising never to return.

Cathy remains on at the Linton home as a guest and while there meets the polite and charming Edgar Linton. Before long, Edgar is a regular caller at Wuthering Heights and a deep friendship begins to develop between Edgar and Cathy.

Heathcliff, meanwhile, has stayed at Wuthering Heights despite his vow to leave. He remains a moody, hovering figure in the background of their lives. Cathy, as attracted as she is to Edgar's kindness and social grace, still retains a passion for the common stable boy. She tries to make something of a gentleman of Heathcliff but he rejects her best efforts.

After a violent quarrel between Heathcliff and Edgar, a quarrel precipitated by the underlying tensions which accompany their desires for Cathy, Cathy runs to Ellen Dean, the Earnshaw house-keeper and impulsively declares that she has decided to give serious consideration to marrying Edgar. The housekeeper knows that Cathy does not really mean what she is saying, but the unobserved Heathcliff overhears her declaration and rides wildly away into the heart of a terrible storm. Cathy, realizing that Heathcliff has been listening and still drawn hypnotically to his love, races after him on her horse. While pursuing him she is thrown from the horse. When Edgar finds her the next morning she is very ill.

Cathy is taken to the Linton home to recuperate. Edgar hopes he can erase all thoughts of Heathcliff forever from her mind with his constant attention and kindness. Cathy does fall in love with Edgar and they are married.

They remain happy and prosperous for two years. Suddenly Heathcliff appears again at Wuthering Heights, having become rich and successful in South America. Moreover, he has now become more polished and genteel in appearance.

Heathcliff once again takes hold of Cathy's heart and soul. He avenges himself on his cruel stepbrother Hindley by buying up Hindley's debts and legal obligations and thereby gaining control of Wuthering Heights.

When he learns that Cathy has married Edgar he seeks revenge against them as well by proceeding to woo Edgar's sister Isabella.

Cathy senses the true motives behind his affections for Isabella and tries to warn the impressionable girl. Her sister-in-law, however, accuses Cathy of wanting Heathcliff for herself and dismisses the efforts as proof of Cathy's jealousy.

Cathy then confronts Heathcliff himself and begs him not to harden his heart against her and Edgar. Heathcliff marries Isabella in spite of Cathy's pleas. Isaella soon discovers that Cathy had told her the truth; Heathcliff treats her with such coldness and disdain that her every waking hour with him is filled with misery.

A sudden illness brings Cathy close to death. Isabella almost welcomes the news because she thinks that if Cathy is gone Heathcliff will come to love her. However, when Heathcliff learns that Cathy is dying, he rushes to her bedside. As she lies on her deathbed Cathy admits that she had always loved Heathcliff and no other man. As Edgar enters the room in the company of a doctor Cathy draws her final breath. Heathcliff, barring Edgar and the doctor from her side, warns them to leave her alone. He declares that finally she belongs to him. Heathcliff then turns to the dead Cathy and begs her to be with him always, even in death.

The flashback ends as Ellen Dean finishes her story. A neighbor arrives at the door and announces that he has seen Heathcliff walking on the moors with a woman. Everyone goes with the guest to whom Ellen Dean has been telling her story and they discover Heathcliff's body under Peniston Crag in the very place where he and Cathy played out their make-believe adventures as children. Heathcliff's face bears a smile; his arms are extended as if in an embrace.

In the final scene of the film, Heathcliff and Cathy walk hand-in-hand on a heavenly cloud.

William Wyler got his first chance to see the romantic ending of *Wuthering Heights*, the ending he had refused to film himself, when Goldwyn premiered the picture at the Pantages Theater on April 13, 1939. Although still unhappy with the ending, Wyler had to agree, along with the rest of the audience, that, as a whole, *Wuthering Heights* was a magnificent piece of filmmaking.

The critics were noticeably enthralled with the picture's romanticism and stark beauty.

Frank S. Nugent of the *New York Times* wrote of the film: "Goldwyn at his best. William Wyler has directed it magnificently, surcharging even his lighter moments with an atmosphere of suspense and foreboding, keeping his horror-shadowed narrative moving at a steadily accelerating pace, building absorbingly to its tragic climax. It is unquestionably one of the most distinguished pictures of the year, one of the finest ever produced by Mr. Goldwyn and one you should decide to see."[18]

Howard Barnes of the *Herald-Tribune* said of *Wuthering Heights:*

It has been brought to the screen with great courage and skill. It is at once a fine film and a masterly translation of a literary classic. There is shrewd showmanship in this Samuel Goldwyn production, but it is marked by a rare integrity. In a brilliant and balanced collaboration, scenarist, director, cast and technicians have succeeded in holding the film to a straight, tragic line. It is a moving and notable motion picture in its own right and it is also a challenging example of how effective an honest treatment can be . . . the result is a distinguished and engrossing screen tragedy.[19]

The critical success of the picture was also reflected in numerous accolades from such quarters as the New York Film Critics and the Academy of Motion Picture Arts and Sciences. The New York Film Critics picked it instead of *Gone With the Wind* as the best picture of the year, and it garnered eight nominations from the Academy including Best Picture, Best Director, Best Actor, Best Supporting Actress (Geraldine Fitzgerald), Best Screenplay, Best Original Score, Best Cinematography, and Best Art/Set Decoration.

As a result of the success of *Wuthering Heights*, Laurence Olivier became a major international star.

Perhaps the greatest achievement of *Wuthering Heights* was that it attempted to combine the elite, or high, culture represented by the Brontë novel and the world of popular entertainment. Goldwyn and his screenwriters knew that the experiences of the audience were limited and that the purpose of popular culture, of which movies were a part, was to verify those everyday experiences. Popular culture aimed to reassure audiences with dramatic situations and characters familiar and comfortable in terms of their everyday lives. Popular culture ordinarily does not attempt to challenge the beliefs or values of the audience.

Goldwyn was aware that to try to challenge his audiences with ideas and values they were unwilling to accept was an impossible task. And yet he knew that great stories like *Wuthering Heights* were not reaching and enriching the lives of theatergoers and exposing them to a world alien to their everyday activities. The average theatergoer undoubtedly would find the manners and customs of Heathcliff and Cathy as strange as the very otherworldly moor they inhabit, yet Goldwyn saw in this world a dramatic core as basic as the rawest emotions of people anywhere.

As in *Dodsworth* he recognized that he could make a film which was not only popular with mass audiences but which would also introduce those audiences to the great literary classics, books which he himself had loved as a young man hungry for culture. Perhaps, Goldwyn mused, the seeing of *Wuthering Heights* would lead to the reading of *Wuthering Heights* and from there to other serious novels. Goldwyn undoubtedly believed that it was worth taking the chance to try to entertain and broaden at the same time.

The themes in *Wuthering Heights* were basic and believable. At the core was the theme of love as obsession. Heathcliff and Cathy are both trapped by their own emotions. For Cathy, there exists a basic bewilderment and confusion about what her true feelings are. She undoubtedly knows and feels in her heart that Edgar is right for her. Yet Heathcliff's spell goes beyond heart and mind and controls her very being. She cannot break free from him even when she wants to. When Heathcliff overhears her tell the housekeeper that she will marry Edgar, he rides out into the stormy night, and Cathy is compelled to run after him. The words expressing her love for Edgar are barely past her lips when she finds herself in flight after Heathcliff. Yet she *does* love Edgar. It is not a self-deception nor is it a ploy to make Heathcliff jealous.

Heathcliff, too, suffers from the malady of love, and it drives him to the brink of madness. He loves Cathy more than he loves his own life. He is willing to sacrifice anything to have her. When Hindley unleashes his viciousness on "the Gypsy scum," Heathcliff is willing to bear it because he knows that if he cannot bear it he will suffer an estrangement from Cathy which would be a far worse agony for him than anything Hindley could conceive. Later, when he is spurned by the Lintons, his pride is hurt. When he departs in a rage vowing never to return it is not for a wounded pride alone but because he has been separated from Cathy. From that moment not only physical distance but social distance as well stands between them. From that moment love for Cathy is not merely remote, it is impossible.

It is this loss which sends Heathcliff reeling into the night like a wounded beast. When he returns from South America successful and refined he seems to have turned into a different man. Yet beneath the fine linen and the polished shoes there still lurks the animallike lover. Heathcliff has not sought out and made his fortune to impress the Lintons or even himself, for he has always thought he was worthy of Cathy. His only motivation for possessing the accoutrements of a gentleman is to reunite him with his true love.

After he has become wealthy and respectable he can see no further roadblocks in his path, and so when he learns that Cathy has married Edgar, his frustration and bitterness drive him to lash out in every direction. His love turns: if he cannot have Cathy he will destroy her and all those around her. Implicit in his thoughts of Cathy's death is his own death wish, for he knows that a life without Cathy would not be worth living.

Heathcliff is not evil, but neither is he sane. His mind works like that of an animal which has been abused by its master. He does not hate Isabella, but when he sees her usefulness as a means to his ends he feels no compunction about hurting her.

Neither does he hate Edgar, despite the fact that, indirectly, Edgar is the cause of Heathcliff's grief. Edgar's kindness for Cathy has no second edge; it was not intended to drive Heathcliff from her. Despite Edgar's intentions Heathcliff interprets the actions in his own way. So obsessed is Heathcliff with ownership of Cathy (for anything less is not genuine love to him) that he does not see that Edgar has brought Cathy far more happiness than he could.

In the end, with Cathy's death, Heathcliff's fury is not so much spent as left directionless. There was only one more course of action to take, and, for Heathcliff it is the proper one. He understands that with her death Cathy is safely in another world where no further harm can come to her. When Heathcliff embraces death he is in effect embracing a new beginning, for at that point nothing could stand in the way of their being together.

When Goldwyn presented the tragedy of Heathcliff and Cathy to American audiences, he sensed that these characters would come as alive for them as they had for him. In *Wuthering Heights*, after all, he gave life and hope to star-crossed lovers, a concept so human and basic that no audience, no matter how ill-read, could easily dismiss. Goldwyn knew that when audiences left the theater they would carry the imprint of Cathy and Heathcliff on their minds for a long time.

The Little Foxes (1941)

The year 1940 had not been a good one for Goldwyn pictures. *The Westerner* and the *Raffles* remake with David Niven had been disappointments. In 1941 Goldwyn was anxious to return to his most successful genre, the adaptation of a literary classic. Once again he turned to the work of one of his favorite authors, Lillian Hellman, and to her play *The Little Foxes.*

Goldwyn sought out his cast and crew with the meticulousness now expected of him. William Wyler, who had directed the earlier Hellman work *These Three* with a good deal of empathy and skill, was the clear choice for director. Lillian Hellman was called on to adapt her own play (with the help of three co-workers including Dorothy Parker, the well-known satirist).

The casting, however, presented more of a problem. The central character, a cruel and ambitious Southern woman named Regina Giddens, had been played on Broadway by Tallulah Bankhead, but she had made no films for almost ten years. Censors—then at the height of their power—also associated her with six sensational films like *Tarnished Lady* that she had made in pre-Production Code days. Both Goldwyn and William Wyler thought that Bette Davis would be the best actress for the part, perhaps the only actress well-known to moviegoers who could do the role justice. Getting Davis was not very easy. It involved trading off stars, a common practice of the time between Hollywood moguls.

The story of how Bette Davis was obtained begins with Jesse Lasky, Goldwyn's ex-brother-in-law. Lasky, down on his luck and desperate, had convinced Jack L. Warner to finance a production of *Sergeant York.* Both agreed that the movie's success would depend on perfect casting. To Warner that meant getting Gary Cooper to play the title role. Cooper, however, was under contract to Samuel Goldwyn, with whom Lasky was not on the best of terms. After some initial hesitation, Lasky called Goldwyn to ask for Cooper's services. To Lasky's utter surprise Goldwyn agreed immediately because, unknown to Lasky, a pending lawsuit was preventing Goldwyn from using Cooper even though the star was still under contract and still drawing a hefty salary. Lasky dutifully told Warner of his success with Goldwyn and Warner called Goldwyn to thank him. Goldwyn mentioned in reply that it would be nice if Warner loaned him Bette Davis. Warner was reluctant to agree until he was finally convinced by Hal Wallis, his production head, that *Sergeant York* could not be made without Cooper.

So Goldwyn got his actress. For a while, however, he almost wished he had not. In 1929, Goldwyn had given Davis a screen test, and at the time he concluded that he liked neither her looks nor her

94   SAMUEL GOLDWYN

voice. Over the years Davis had not forgotten this snub, and as the filming of *The Little Foxes* approached she decided to ask for the unheard of sum of $385,000.

After a considerable amount of histrionics from both parties, Goldwyn agreed to the sum. This was not uncharacteristic of Goldwyn: money was always secondary if an artist was needed for a particular role. When filming started, Davis took up with Wyler where she had left off with Goldwyn. Her conception of how the main character was to be played differed markedly from both Goldwyn's and Wyler's. Wyler recalls:

She thought I was making her play the part like Tallulah Bankhead. I was not. It was the story of this woman who was greedy and high-handed but a woman of great poise, great charm, great wit. And that's the way Talullah had played it on the stage. But Bette Davis was playing it all like a villain because she had been playing bitches and parts like that—this is what made her at Warner Brothers—Jezebel and things like that, but she was playing Regina with no shading . . . all the villainy and greediness of the part but not enough of the charm and wit and humor and sexiness of this woman. So, anyway, she thought when I tried to correct her that I was trying to make her imitate Tallulah Bankhead which I was not. And she was also trying to make herself look older because she had a daughter of nineteen in the story who was played by Teresa Wright. And it's true . . . perhaps she wasn't quite old enough but it wasn't necessary to play a character part either. I wanted her to be more attractive, more sexy. This is often the case with actors and actresses. They don't like to play their age. They don't mind playing ten years older or younger but not their exact age.[20]

The fighting continued right through the making of the film. At one point Bette Davis even walked off the set. Goldwyn, making use of a fine print clause in her contract, which stated that if she were unable to finish the picture for a reason other than ill health that she was liable for all production costs, finally got his temperamental actress in front of the camera again.

This, however, was his only victory, for Davis refused to change her interpretation of Regina Giddens, though Wyler persisted in his efforts right up to the final day of shooting. When the picture opened most critics agreed that Wyler had been right and that Davis had played the part too broadly and with little subtlety.

The story in *The Little Foxes* takes place in the South at the turn of the last century. The story concerns the Hubbard clan and their desire for wealth and power. Regina Hubbard Giddens is approached by her two brothers, Ben and Oscar, to go into business. They need $75,000 more to build a cotton mill and take advantage of the ready supply of cheap labor. Regina sees this offer as an opportunity to make herself rich.

She plays up to a Northern financier named William Marshall, the brothers' partner, and arranges a dinner party for him with the idea of sizing him up. Regina then sends her daughter Alexandra to Baltimore to bring back Horace, Regina's banker-husband. Horace has been in a sanitarium recovering from a heart attack.

Despite Regina's constant pressure, Horace insists that he has no intention of investing in such a venture as the mill. Ben and Oscar, who cannot wait any longer, decide to seek the necessary funds elsewhere. They get Oscar's son Leo, who works in the family bank, to steal enough of Horace's negotiable bonds to make up the difference.

Regina learns of the theft and decides to blackmail her brothers into giving her part ownership of the business. Horace, though, as a way to spite Regina, insists that the securities were given to Leo of

A couple on a deadly course: Herbert Marshall and Bette Davis in The Little Foxes.

his own free will as a kind of loan. Regina is enraged by what she considers Horace's treachery. She baits her husband and badgers him until he has another heart attack. Then, as he is dying, she refuses to help him, or even to give him his medicine. When he collapses while struggling to climb the stairs she finally calls for the servants. As he lies on his deathbed Regina taunts him further and defies him to incriminate her. Instead, Horace tries to comfort his daughter and warns her to escape from the evil influence of her mother by marrying David Hewitt, a young newspaper editor before her mother pushes her into a loveless marriage with her cousin Leo.

After her husband's death Regina becomes even more brazen in her attempt to gain a foothold in her brothers' fledgling company. She promises not to say anything about Leo's theft of her late husband's securities if she is given two thirds of the business.

When Alexandra overhears her mother's ultimatum, she, for the first time, truly sees the real viciousness in her mother and denounces Regina, saying that she cannot bear to live in the same house with her. Alexandra runs away with David, who has been waiting outside in the rain.

As Regina watches them walk away, she is seen as a woman possessing everything she had set out to get, but in her quest, she has lost or isolated herself from everyone who might have loved her.

The theme of family discord was familiar to Goldwyn. He had presented it in such earlier films as *Cynara, The Wedding Night,* and *Dodsworth.* This time, however, the agent which causes strife is not the marital institution itself, but the pressures of society, or even simple lust. In *The Little Foxes* it is Regina herself who single-handedly undermines the lives and relationships of an otherwise normal and healthy family. Regina's brothers are merely trying to live out the American Dream by entering into business; although admittedly they are not cast as angels, since they plan to exploit the workers by giving them menial wages and because they are willing to play with the company books to insure success.

Regina, reminiscent of Heathcliff in her single-minded determination to get what she wants, is willing to use blackmail and murder to accomplish her goals.

As the family disintegrates because of Regina's evil machinations, Alexandra remains the only family member untouched by the destructive chain of events. Through no fault of her own, Alexandra's own happiness is threatened by the continuing erosion of the family. Her impending marriage to Leo would trap her permanently in her mother's web of hateful deceits.

It is not accidental that Goldwyn uses the character of David Hewitt as Alexandra's salvation. Although the genders have been reversed from the situation in *Dodsworth*, in which Edith Cortwright allows Sam Dodsworth an escape from his unhappy family situation, the elements of that salvation are the same. When Alexandra learns of her mother's blackmail plans and Regina's part in the death of Alexandra's father, Alexandra knows she can find escape and real love now only outside her family in the person of David.

Goldwyn's message in both *Dodsworth* and *The Little Foxes* is that the institution of the family is and should be held in the highest regard, as should the institution of marriage. However, when a family or a marriage is so destructive as to endanger the very lives of the people affected, it is then acceptable to seek a new life through a new marriage or a new family.

The ending of *The Little Foxes*, like that of *Dodsworth*, is an optimistic one. Unlike *The Wedding Night*, in which Tony is allowed only a vision of Manya, or *Wuthering Heights*, in which the audience must be content with the belief that the love of Heathcliff and Cathy has survived in another dimension, Alexandra and David go out with hope to face a living world and to rebuild for themselves and their progeny the happiness which is now gone from her mother's house.

6

Popular Entertainment, Popular Art

AT THE CENTER OF GOLDWYN'S CONCEPTION of an artist's mission was the realization that the creation of art, the choice of subject, of form, was only part of the artist's task. Beyond the actual creation of the work of art lay the equally difficult problem of presenting that art to others. While some art is conceived and executed only for the pleasure of the artist or a small group of people, Goldwyn's artistic interest in the common person as subject matter was matched by his interest in having as many common people as possible see his art.

In his mind art was not truly art until it was seen by many. This is in part a commercial conceptualization, not one, however, defined by profits, but by an inner satisfaction that the art one has created is seen by many people. There is still a bit of Goldwyn the glove salesman in Goldwyn the film distributor, but it is a salesman peddling a genuine product.

Goldwyn's acute awareness of his audience's tastes—which he identified with his own—accompanied by his own artistic views, led him to make "popular" art using a "popular" medium. Popular art is not evident only in his musicals and in his comedies but in his melodramas and in his most serious work. One of the major arguments against viewing Goldwyn as an important artist, in fact, is that he was merely a creator of popular entertainments, rather than a creator of genuine art.

In general, it is possible to distinguish among three types of art: folk art, popular art, and high art. Folk art tends to be simple, to be created by the artist for personal pleasure, or to provide pleasure to family and friends. The folk artist seeks neither money nor fame in creating. Examples of folk art are a musician sitting on a porch in Texas playing a guitar or a soap carver sculpting a boat. Popular art is created by the artist for personal pleasure but also as a commercial

Danny Kaye with Constance Dowling in Up in Arms.

product to be sold. The popular artist usually seeks money and/or fame. Because the popular artist seeks recognition the artist must appeal to large numbers of people or else the art will be withdrawn from sale in favor of an artistic product which will sell better. Examples of popular art are the makers of television shows, and movie producers. High art tends to appeal to a much smaller, generally more intellectual group of people, than popular art. The success of the high artist is not against the actual or potential commercial successes of competitive artistic products but instead is measured against an accepted body of classics in the field of art in which the artist creates. Thus, a high art novelist is measured against Flaubert and Tolstoy while a popular novelist is measured against best-selling novelists.

Because the popular artist is measured by sales, that artist tends to create products which reflect the values held by the audience and to confirm the validity of those values. Since high art generally is less concerned with commercial success than attaining a place in artistic history the values of the audience need not be reflected; indeed, those values can be and often are frontally challenged.

Of course these divisions are crude, and it is often the case that a work of art seems to fit all of these categories, or two of them. An especially difficult borderline to ascertain lies between popular and high art.

Critics of Goldwyn films, such as James Agee in his analysis of *The Best Years of Our Lives*, imply that Goldwyn's mediocre films are merely diverting entertainment useful only in passing time, and his best films are only polished, expensive works chiefly interesting to the middle class for whom the films were made, but unworthy of being placed in the cinematic high-art tradition started by D. W. Griffith.

Against such claims Goldwyn defenders have two lines of argument. One is the films themselves. One can argue how many times Goldwyn challenged the audience's values. The second line of argument is that the attack on Goldwyn as a maker of popular films is, in fact, not really an attack on Goldwyn but on the whole of popular art.

Without design or intention Goldwyn emerges as a champion of popular culture. Richard Griffith, in discussing *The Best Years of Our Lives*, sums up what popular art does: ". . . it shows representative Americans as they are, presents their problems as they themselves see them, and provides only such solutions—partial, temporary, personal—as they themselves would accept. The picture's values are the values of the people in it . . . the contempt for this drama of the ordinary seemed to be in reality a contempt for the ordinary itself."[1]

To degrade popular art is to dismiss the feelings of the mass of people. If their ideas and values are derivative, if their behavior is unsophisticated, or if their sentiments too quickly aroused, that is not the fault of the artist portraying people belonging to that mass. The art can only, at its best, mirror and then try to explain.

Democratic thinkers must ponder the tastes and habits of the public, and democratic artists must come face to face with popular culture. It is not surprising that critics of popular culture are also antidemocratic, preferring high art in an autocracy.

Goldwyn's contribution to the development of popular art was to develop the taste of the masses. Critics of popular art thought popular art inevitably reduced the artistic taste and would, in time, destroy all high art. Against such general claims (as made, for example, in Ortega y Gassett's *Revolt of the Masses* [1930] or T. S. Eliot's *Notes Toward a Definition of Culture* [1948]) comes a defense provided by Goldwyn's films.

Cinematically a Goldwyn film is equal to one by Welles, Bergman, or Fellini. His themes, however, are completely different. Goldwyn chose stories of ordinary people in dramatic situations. By contrast, the other filmmakers often filmed extraordinary, or highly unusual, characters in psychological situations beyond the normal imagination.

It is pointless to argue that one of these approaches is truer art than the other; there is certainly room for both. Goldwyn's achievement is that he justifies high art's making that room for popular art because, as Goldwyn proves, popular art is capable of high achievement.

This achievement was reached by Goldwyn in his best films. There are, in addition to his serious work of art, many lighter pieces of entertainment. It is possible to dismiss the musicals, the comedies, and the adventure-mystery films by saying that Goldwyn meant no more for them than is contained in the notion of entertainment: to divert attention from the difficulties of daily life by providing amusement.

Because Goldwyn told stories about ordinary people in his serious movies, it is certainly likely that his understanding of them included an acknowledgment that their lives were indeed difficult, that entertainment, even in its crudest sense, as defined, was very much a needed part of their lives. Goldwyn made his popular entertainments not just to make money, not just to tread water between serious film, but to provide entertainment to the same audiences he attempted to enlighten in more serious works.

In this dual manner—providing entertainment and instruction—Goldwyn emerges as a genuinely popular entertainer.

Because the entertainment pieces did not have a moral purpose for Goldwyn, it is important to determine the sorts of material with which he chose to do that entertaining. The popular entertainment films form a large part of Goldwyn's career and they, as much as the serious films, deserve extended mention.

Unlike films exploring serious themes, there is little unity to be found in the popular entertainments. They may be subdivided by genre, but each really exists on its own in most respects.

The Eddie Cantor Films

From 1930 until 1936 Samuel Goldwyn produced six films which starred the pop-eyed, and popular, comedian Eddie Cantor—*Whoopee!* (1930), *Palmy Days* (1931), *The Kid from Spain* (1932), *Roman Scandals* (1933), *Kid Millions* (1934), and *Strike Me Pink* (1936). They were all made as Goldwyn prepared to make a screen version of Florenz Ziegfeld's follies, a version eventually made as *The Goldwyn Follies* (1938). Goldwyn had decided that Depression audiences needed an uplift. They wanted music, they wanted to laugh, to forget the world outside the theater. In his desire to provide this, Goldwyn joined up with Flo Ziegfeld (the first and only time Goldwyn had a partner since becoming an independent producer).

He decided to buy the film rights to Ziegfeld's successful musical *Whoopee!* and to hire Eddie Cantor, the star of the Broadway play, to play the lead in the movie. Goldwyn was fascinated by the spectacle of the original with its horses, its bevy of Indian maidens wearing very little clothing, its comic sketches and extravagant dance numbers.

To duplicate the complete sense of the original Goldwyn went beyond Cantor and got both Ziegfeld and Busby Berkeley, the choreographer, to help him. (*Whoopee!* was the first film which included Berkeley's patented shots of dancers, from above and from many other angles.) After some legal battles Goldwyn was also able to obtain the screenwriting services of William Anthony McGuire who had written the original.

Part of the attraction of any Ziegfeld show, and *Whoopee!* was no exception, was the collection of beautiful women. In Hollywood Goldwyn chose the actresses who were thereafter known as the Goldwyn Girls. At the beginning the group included such soon-to-be well-known names as Paulette Goddard and Virginia Bruce. Betty Grable is also in the picture.

The film itself is built around Eddie Cantor's style of comedy, and many of the scenes in the film are really film versions of burlesque sketches (such as Cantor's famous one when, dressed as an Indian, he is trying to sell his wares). The story is that of a hypochondriac from the East named Henry Williams. Henry takes pills to calm his nerves and is out in Arizona relaxing on a ranch accompanied by a nurse, Mary Custer. At the ranch he meets a pretty girl named Sally Morgen. Sally is to marry the sheriff of the town, Bob Wells, but Sally is in love with an Indian named Wanenis. Henry manages to arrange it so Sally and Wanenis get together. At the end of the film it is revealed by Wanenis', Indian parents, that, in fact, Wanenis is white, that he was left as a baby and raised by the Indians.

Whoopee! was a triumph for Eddie Cantor. "In addition to dispensing [his] style of comedy, Cantor sang his trademark song, Making Whoopee, as well as Baby Just Cares for Me, did one of his patented blackface routines . . . , " and solidified "his screen image as . . . a nervous, timid"[2] character. Almost all the critics loved the film. Mordaunt Hall thought: "Mr. Cantor's clowing transcends even Mr. Ziegfeld's shining beauties, the clever direction and the tuneful melodies, and this is saying a great deal, for there is much for the eyes to feast on . . . this results in the film being a swift and wonderfully entertaining offering, a feature that should prove to motion picture chieftains that such attractions are well worth all the trouble taken in production, despite the subordinating of the popular romantic theme."[3] Hall's praise is not excessive. In fact, Miles Kruger believes *Whoopee!* to be "an ideal time capsule, preserving better than any other screen musical the flavor and style of Broadway musicals during the late 1920s."[4] Despite Goldwyn's lack of musical knowledge *Whoopee!* was an enormous financial success as well, so much a success Goldwyn decided to continue the Cantor films. Goldwyn liked the basic idea of *Whoopee!* enough to refurbish it fourteen years after the original as *Up in Arms* and give the lead to Danny Kaye.

Goldwyn's musical inadequacies are worth underscoring for they haunted him. He was able to understand and control virtually every other aspect of the making of a film but never, to his final film, would he master the musical. As Arthur Marx has written: "He may have had instinctive genius for putting his famed Goldwyn Touch on every other end of the business—costumes, settings, characters, dialogue, plot construction, and publicity, but when it came to music, every composer who worked for him swore he knew nothing. . . ."[5]

Whoopee! had developed a formula, however, and Goldwyn was to use it again and again. The musical was some kind of giant pot into which was thrown good-tasting elements which, in theory, should produce a good-tasting whole. In fact, this theory often proved false, but audiences were not there for theories; they sat in theaters waiting for Eddie Cantor or Bob Hope or Danny Kaye to entertain them.

After *Palmy Days*, Cantor, in 1932, went to work on *The Kid from Spain*. In this film Cantor was reunited with the Goldwyn Girls and Busby Berkeley. Leo McCarey was brought in to direct. (On

Troubadour Eddie Cantor in The Kid from Spain. *(Courtesy: Museum of Modern Art/Film Stills Archive)*

the basis of *The Kid from Spain,* the Marx Brothers hired McCarey to direct *Duck Soup.*)

The film's plot—typical of the absurdities of film musicals of the 1930s—involves two college students, Eddie Williams and Ricardo, his Mexican roommate (played by Robert Young). The two are found in a girl's dormitory and are expelled. Ricardo convices Eddie to come with him to Mexico. Eddie agrees and they go to a bank so that Ricardo can get his money. While waiting outside for his friend to return, Eddie is joined in the car by a group of bank robbers who mistake Eddie for the getaway driver. Fearing the wrath of the thieves when they find out he is not who they thought, Eddie crosses the border into Mexico. At the border Eddie must disguise himself as a Mexican in order to get past the guard. Once in Mexico Eddie is again mistakenly identified but this time as Don Sebastian's son (Don Sebastian was a famed bullfighter). Eddie keeps this identity when he discovers that Crawford, an American law enforcement agent, is keeping track of him. Eddie travels to his friend Ricardo's house and discovers that Ricardo is in love with Anita Gomez. Pancho, a noted matador, is also in love with Anita, and it is Pancho who Anita's father wishes her to marry. Eddie, in seeking to help plead Ricardo's case, meets Anita's friend Rosalie who likes him. Rosalie is liked, in turn, by Pancho's friend Pedro. With Crawford convinced that he is in disguise, Eddie has to accept the challenge of fighting a bull. Ricardo promises the bull will be calm, will, in fact, simply stop when it hears the word "Popocatepetl," a word Eddie has some trouble remembering. At the bullring, however, Pedro replaces the ringer bull with a very mean bull. The bull and Eddie chase each other around the ring until Eddie finally subdues it with chloroform. After this fight Eddie wins Rosalie, and Ricardo and Anita are united.

Reviewers still liked the formula, even while recognizing it for what it was. As the reviewer in *Time* wrote, "If you like Eddie Cantor, you'll probably like this picture in which, surrounded by prettier girls than usual, he performs throughly typical Cantor antics while rolling his popeyes and giving exaggerated gulps."[6]

Roman Scandals, with Cantor as a Roman slave in Nero's reign trying to avoid being eaten by a lion in the Coliseum, was notable not for any new element in the formula but for the introduction of Lucille Ball as a Goldwyn Girl. (Her clowning on and off the set lead to Goldwyn's decision to let her go after her contract expired.)

Following *Roman Scandals* Goldwyn made *Kid Millions,* again with a formula story about the standard Cantor character who inherits seventy-seven million dollors and plans to use his new fortune to build an ice cream factory where children with no money can eat all the ice cream they want to. One sequence in the film involves a skating rink made of ice cream. Goldwyn decided to use Technicolor to shoot the sequence which, with the possible exception of Walt Disney cartoons, made the best use of color of any film of its day.

With *Strike Me Pink*, the formula simply ran out of energy. Like all the other Cantor films, *Strike Me Pink* was a success, but both the public and the critics were tired of the same gift in different packages. Goldwyn decided after the film's reception to discontinue Eddie Cantor Films (although Cantor continued to make occasional films for other producers until 1948).

Those early musical-comedy-entertainment films were important for Goldwyn. On the simplest level they were financially very successful. Their success, and the success of many of Goldwyn's other purely "entertainment" pictures, though, should be seen in their proper context. Goldwyn, having made money, could have gone simply making more of the general type of pictures, albeit with different stars and different formulae. Instead he chose another way. "Many a director has made 'one for the box office' in order to gain the freedom to make one for himself. Mr. Goldwyn is the only producer known to have set out to finance expensive experiments with the profits of lush musicals."[7] Goldwyn did not make entertainment pictures solely to provide fun for the filmgoing public, or to fill the Goldwyn coffers. He needed the money to make the films he wanted, and, equally important, the films he believed his audiences really needed. Ironically, these very entertainment musicals which were so liberating for Goldwyn finally were the type of films on which he foundered. He became angered over his inability to conquer them, and despite the fact that they were not considered on the same critical plane as his more serious films, he considered it just as important for him to make them as artistically successful as those serious films. He never gave up trying to do this, and he never succeeded.

Woman Chases Man (1937)

During the 1930s a new kind of comedy emerged, noted for its emphasis on dialogue and slapstick. Movies such as *It Happened One Night* started the subgenre known as the "screwball" comedy.

Why did such comedies emerge? Lewis Jacobs has noted that "The loss of credibility in former values, the breakdown of the smugness and self-confidence of the jazz era, the growing bewilderment and dissatifaction in a 'crazy' world that does not make sense, has been reflected in a revival of comedies of satire and self-ridicule."[8] Such self-satirization appealed to Goldwyn who had used it before in such films as *Potash and Perlmutter* and *Bulldog Drummond*. Goldwyn was also interested in the sexually liberating undertones of the "screwball" comedy insofar as they complemented his own gropings in his dramas of adultery.

The loosening of sexual attitudes, both obvious and flippantly presented in these comedies, began after World War I. During the twenty-five years preceding the outbreak of World War I life had been changed by all kinds of inventions: the airplane, the automobile, the phonograph, motion picture, and the pioneering though impractical experiments in television, among many others. The result of this explosion in technology, when virtually every modern communication and transportation medium was developed, was a great optimism. The inventions provided hope that human beings were on the verge of being able to solve all their problems. People could see progress, and rapid progress at that, right in front of them; they could not doubt its reality and they did not doubt its effectiveness. The development of motion pictures, for example, was hailed as the beginning of the first universal language (because, of course, movies were silent and so no particular national language could be used). This language, it was hoped, would lead to world peace because people would be able to see accurate images of life in other cultures and would no longer be afraid of foreign peoples they never saw and whose way of life they could not understand. In such a rarefied atmosphere of optimism people worked hard believing they had almost won their struggle.

World War I disturbed this view, ending the optimistic view of human nature as capable of improvement and human society as being perfectible. In society this sudden fall from innocence, this troubling view of the persistence of evil in human nature and social forms, led to a decadence epitomized by the Jazz Age of gangsters, bootleggers, and advocates of free love (such as the flamboyant dancer Isadora Duncan). On screen this letting go, this dismissal of traditional modes of behavior, was devastating. Audiences after the war would not sit through D. W. Griffith's Victorian melodramas of chaste women and Old World values.

Half of the "screwball" comedy is derived from this letting go. The other half, as Jacobs suggests, comes from a reaction to the Depression world of the 1930s, a world in which the excesses of the Jazz Age disappeared, to be replaced by a world of harsh economic conditions. The Depression generation "felt cheated of its birthright and apprehensively faced further loss in the steady approach of war . . . a world of frustration was mirrored in them [screwball comedies]."[9] The deprivation of the Depression coupled with the legacy of sexual liberation coming from the previous decade led to the rise of this special comedy.

Samuel Goldwyn made only one real contribution to "screwball" comedy. It was a picture he himself regarded as a major failure, a judgment with which most critics were eager to agree. Yet *Woman Chases Man,* seen. at a distance, had considerable merit and even significance. It deserves more attention than it has received.

The making of the film involved one miscalculation after another. The screenplay was worked on by three people. Dissatisfied with the result, Goldwyn gave it to Eddie Chodorov, a playwright. Chodorov read it and found the script so unsatisfactory he refused to work on it. Goldwyn kept the script and looked for a director. Goldwyn wanted William Wyler to direct the picture but Wyler refused after reading the script. Wyler did end up working on the film for a few weeks but then withdrew in favor of John Blystone who had directed comedies and Westerns. Blystone was not used, however, to stories about the cheated young anxious to find what could respectably pass for success or love, so he stuck closely to the script with its series of plots and counterplots centering on sex, love, and money.

Woman Chases Man is the story of a father and son and the effect on their lives of the arrival of a young woman. The son, Kenneth Nolan (Joel McCrea), is a millionaire who is very conservative when it comes to spending his money. Kenneth is sought by Nina Tennyson who is poor. She does not love Kenneth; in fact, she intends to leave him after their marriage in order to marry the man she really loves, the man she passes off as her uncle.

Kenneth's father, B. J. Nolan (Charles Winninger) is in financial trouble. Deeply in debt, he needs $100,000 quickly in order to build a suburban development called Nolan Heights. Into B. J.'s office walks Virginia (Miriam Hopkins) an aggressive architect hampered by the depression and by the fact that she is female. She informs B. J. that her blueprints will insure the success of Nolan Heights. He is willing to listen, telling her of his financial state and the sad fact that his own son will not lend him the needed funds. Out of work and desperate, Virginia strikes a deal with B. J.: he agrees that if he is somehow able to get the money then she will build the development. Smelling the success she has dreamed about, Virginia gets two unemployed friends named Hunk and Judy to assist her in getting Kenneth to give his father a loan. Disguised as butler and maid, they are meant to convince Kenneth of his father's success. When Virginia sees Kenneth her aim widens to include capturing him as well. Kenneth seems to have novices and his fiancée seems opposed to giving the loan. Thus Virginia must expose the romance for the sham that it is while finding Kenneth's weak spot. She does both when she discovers that Kenneth likes to drink. She makes him so drunk that he signs a contract. The two end up on a tree where, eventually, Kenneth learns the true nature of Nina and is reunited with his father.

Stripped of its comedy *Woman Chases Man* is very similar to other Goldwyn films about love and marriage: a man on the verge of being married leaves the woman he was about to marry, who is no good for him, and goes instead to an attractive, younger woman who revitalizes his sense of life. This is remarkably close to the basic idea in *Cynara* and *Dodsworth*. The difference here is the comedy which virtually completely covers the underlying message, that sexual passion can result in happiness. Virginia Travis is animated by a dual lust: for money and for Kenneth. The same might be said about Nina Tennyson except that Virginia's lust for Kenneth is greater than her lust for money, and her lust is identified with romantic love. Still, sexual feelings as the basis for human motivation are basic to the movement of the plot. In Graham Greene's words about the film: "Sex isn't sublimated." Instead sexual passion is allowed to be presented as a genuine human feeling, one which should not be repressed.

Additionally, *Woman Chases Man* provides a sympathetic portrait of a generation's angry young people, without jobs but not without the quick wits necessary for survival. The movie was meant to be seen by these young people who felt the strains of sexual liberation and who identified with the struggling Hunk and Judy as well as Virginia.

In making the film, as pure entertainment, therefore, Goldwyn made an error. There is a serious story about a serious subject in *Woman Chases Man*, and there is a comedy which, to work, needed more defined characterizations, and a more believable plot. Trying

Joel McCrea and Miriam Hopkins at a high point of Goldwyn's screwball comedy,
Woman Chases Man.

to cross genres does not work here. Howard Barnes, in a typical
critical notice, asserts that "*Woman Chases Man* is spun out of the
sheerest nonsense. It throws daffy characters together in daffy
situations and gives them glib, amusing speech. Unfortunately,
farcical invention runs thin before the ending and the show goes
over into rather strained slapstick." [10] Critics did praise the production values, the direction (despite, it was said, the weak script with
which to work), and many of the performances. What critics did not
notice—because they were reviewing what was meant to be and was
billed as a purely entertaining film—was how accurately *Woman
Chases Man* summed up the feeling of an entire generation of
Americans. In Richard Griffith's words, "Contemporary criticism
dismissed it as a trifle light as air, something for the silly season. It
weighed a good deal more than that, however, to those who were
young in the thirties." [11]

The Goldwyn Follies (1938)

Samuel Goldwyn had first worked with Florenz Ziegfeld in the
making of *Whoopee!* Goldwyn had long admired Ziegfeld's Follies

and sought for a comparable motion picture extravaganza on a yearly basis. Goldwyn worked on the idea for a number of years, with the project constantly being delayed. When Ziegfeld died in 1932 Goldwyn seized the moment to announce that the Follies tradition would not be allowed to die. Although Goldwyn himself had little experience in the making of musicals, RKO, MGM, Universal, and Twentieth-Century Fox had all had their share of musical hits.

Goldwyn realized that his first and most crucial task was to obtain a usable script with enough latitude in it to allow for all the variety acts needed in a review of the Follies type. Goldwyn sought that script from a variety of places. First he had Harry Selby, a journalist from New York. Selby was soon followed by Harry J. Green and the writer Alice Duer Miller (working with Bert Kalmar and Harry Ruby). Soon after that, Kamar and Ruby went back to Harry J. Green to work with him. This trio was followed by the husband and wife team of Dorothy 'Parker and Alan Campbell, and then another such marital team, Anita Loos and John Emerson. Goldwyn had paid about $125,000 for the original script which was, in turn, altered by each of these writers. By the time the film was ready for production Goldwyn had reviewed nearly a dozen scripts and rejected them all. Desperately, he looked about for someone who worked both quickly and well. He came up with Ben Hecht (whose name appears alone on the screen credits). Hecht, knowing Goldwyn wanted results, finished a script in two weeks.

In an attempt to obtain an international flavor, Goldwyn tried to secure the directorial skills of French director René Clair, perhaps best known for his work *À Nous La Liberte* (1931). Clair "worked with a minimum of dialogue, using music, choruses and sound effects to counterpoint and comment upon his visuals. In this principle of asynchronous sound, sound used against rather than with the images."[12] Goldwyn wanted a director known for his special abilities in raising music beyond the entertainment level into the world of art. Clair, however, was not enthusiastic about the project, evidently seeing no worthwhile visuals against which to counterpoint the Hollywood production numbers Goldwyn described to him. Finally Goldwyn engaged the talents of George Marshall (assisted, though without credit, by H. C. Potter).

A musical must first of all be measured by its music and so, in typical fashion, Goldwyn set out ot get the best. George and Ira Gershwin were hired to write the score, and Vernon Duke to write the ballet music. (George Gershwin completed only four songs in the film—"Love Walked In," "Love is Here to Stay," "I Was Doing All Right," and "I Love to Rhyme"—when he died from a brain tumor on July 11, 1937.) Duke took over Gershwin's place and George's brother Ira continued to supply the lyrics.

Well-known choreographer George Balanchine was brought in to oversee the dance numbers. Goldwyn himself knew nothing at all about dancing or choreography. He relied on experts but was not above changing their suggestions. He had reportedly rejected Martha Graham's participation because he thought that the modern dance in which she specialized not modern enough, and "When Balanchine dreamed up a dance sequence based on Gershwin's *An American in Paris*, Sam threw it out saying it wasn't for motion picture audiences. Later that same ballet became the basis of the Academy Award winner, *An American in Paris*, starring Gene Kelly and Leslie Caron, which MGM produced."[13]

When it came to the music and dance then—the key elements— Goldwyn had had no innate talent and no experience. He was clearly outside his range of talents, and unable to test the precise limits of that range as well as to capitalize on the success of Ziegfeld's work.

To support the main story line Goldwyn hired a series of acts to be interspersed as the story was being told. These specialty acts were performed by such stars as Vera Zorina, George Balanchine's wife and a well-known ballerina, the Ritz Brothers, Bobby Clark of the Metropolitan Opera, the 1938 Goldwyn Girls, and the picture's main success, Edgar Bergen and Charlie McCarthy. The ventriloquist and his dummy were not well known when they were signed to appear in the film, but in the eighteen months that it took to do the film they appeared on radio and attracted a national audience. By the time the film was distributed audiences recognized the familiar routines Bergen performed in the film and greeted them with great enthusiasm. Goldwyn, who never listened to radio, was surprised at the intensity of the reaction, and, until the bad reviews and box-office receipts became known, planned to star Bergen in a whole series of films.

Goldwyn spent two million dollars into the making of his *Follies* (a title that would haunt him and tempt his critics). Besides the hiring of Gershwin, Balanchine, and the various stars Goldwyn decided to make the *Follies* completely in Technicolor, the first time he had done this. (*Whoopee!* was shot in a two-color process.)

The nineteen production numbers in the film interrupted a story of a Hollywood producer and young love. The movie producer in the film is named Oliver Merlin, a purveyor of second-rate movies. During the course of filming, two young women observe the moviemaking process, and one of them, Hazel Dawes, says that "if only it could be simple and human" the movie being made would appear less pretentious and would have more appeal. Merlin overhears her comment and realized that the reason his movies have failed is that he "cannot buy common sense." He hires Hazel—calling her Miss Humanity in publicity—as a simple girl who can instruct him about the ordinary feelings of common people.

During a break from her job Hazel goes into a restaurant to order a hamburger and meets the singing man behind the counter, Danny Beecher. Hazel decides to engineer Danny's success secretly, so that he will be successful enough to marry her but will not think that she is responsible for that success. As Hazel continues to work for Merlin, the producer finds that, despite their age difference, he is falling in love with his advisor. Hazel manages to convince him to hire Danny, though pretending she does not know him. When Merlin observes Danny and Hazel together and sees by the way they look at each other that they are in love he is angry and (uncharacteristically, since he has been very kind to everyone throughout) he threatens to cut Danny from the film and reshoot unless Hazel agrees to become his (Merlin's) wife. Reluctantly, she agrees because she does not want to endanger Danny's chances. Danny then tells her that he wants to marry her whatever the consequences. Merlin, realizing that Hazel does not love him, reverts to his normally kind self and gives up his plans to force the marriage.

Of course there is much self-mockery in this plot of a producer in search of simple stories with honest human emotions. But the story and characters are hardly developed enough—because of the frequent breaks for production numbers—to have a satisfying movie. Some of these production numbers are cute—especially those of the Ritz Brothers—but, with the possible exception of "Love Walked In" (which is sung four times in the film) there is no memorable Gershwin tune. An incomplete story line coupled with second-rate production numbers could not make an entertaining movie.

Goldwyn's old nemesis, providing continuity in a film which mixed several genres, is a problem specifically raised by Frank Nugent, the *New York Times*'s critic. Nugent wrote: "Since it bears the Goldwyn trademark, it goes without saying that it is a superior

hodgepodge, peopled almost exclusively by superior specialists . . .
but none of it . . . has been brought into a semblance of
continuity. . . . On the evidence, it appears that Mr. Goldwyn tossed
the story out to make room for the cast and what's left of the Hecht
plot reduces Andrea Leeds and Adolphe Menjou [who portray Hazel
Dawes and Oliver Merlin] to the status of tourist guides during the
filming of a Hollywood musical." Howard Barnes, joining the
chorus, wrote ". . . it would almost appear as though Mr. Goldwyn
had tried to see just how much could be crammed into that hybrid
form known as the screen musical."[14]

Although the problem of continuity in films of combined genres
would continue to remain essentially unsolved, Goldwyn did, from
time to time, continue to mix the comic and the dramatic and, more
rarely, the dramatic and the musical (as in his last two films, *Guys
and Dolls* and *Porgy and Bess*). Generally, though, Goldwyn was
chastened by his experience with *The Goldwyn Follies*. In one sense
he learned that he could not rely on another's (Ziegfeld's) success to
propel his own, but, more importantly, he learned that the principle
of entertainment in film was not to provide a wide variety of acts
giving everyone in the audience some act to admire, but rather to
provide a story line with continuity, a story that told of the events in
the lives of people with whom the audience could identify. He
learned also that films needed scenes which follow one another
logically and which ultimately could be seen to the cohesive. *The
Goldwyn Follies* emerges as Goldwyn's most ambitious, and one of
his most interesting failures. Along with *Woman Chases Man* it
shows just how slippery the magic Goldwyn touch could be.

Raffles (1940)

In 1930 Samuel Goldwyn had hired Sidney Howard to do a
screenplay based on E. W. Hornung's famous character Raffles.
Ronald Coleman had starred in the very successful film. By 1939
Goldwyn thought that just enough time—and a screen generation—
had passed to allow a remake of *Raffles*. He knew that he wanted
David Niven, who had appeared in such Goldwyn films as *Dodsworth* and *Wuthering Heights*, to take Colman's place as the
protagonist. Additionally, rather than using the old Howard screenplay Goldwyn decided to start fresh. He hired the well-known
author John Van Druten to redo the original screenplay by making
it more modern. Not fully satisfied with Van Druten's finished
product, Goldwyn brought in a number of other authors, including

F. Scott Fitzgerald, to add finishing touches. Goldwyn signed Sam Wood to direct the film, and then sought other well-known stars to support Niven; the best-known was Olivia de Haviland.

The story in the new film remained remarkably similar to the original. The changes—such as the addition of the Scotland Yard inspector observing Raffles at a cricket match over television—seem out of place and obtrusive, as though they were put there simply to justify a modern version of a film made only a decade before. Both films, though, retain the lightheartedness and the adventurousness of the original novel.

Raffles is the story of a thief named A. J. (or Jack) Raffles, who taunts police by leaving his calling card in the safes he has looted, both announcing that it has been his hand again at work and challenging Scotland Yard to capture him. Raffles is in love with a young woman named Gwen Manders and he plans to reform and marry her. Gwen's brother, Bunny, though, is in desperate need of one thousand pounds by the following Monday to cover gambling losses and money which he had stolen.

Seeking to help him out, Raffles decides upon a theft at Bunny's aunt and uncle's (the Melroses) estate. He plans to steal Lady Kittly Melrose's valuable emerald necklace and give it to Bunny—who will then return the necklace, receive the reward, and pay off his debts.

Meanwhile Scotland Yard's Inspector Mackenzie, suspecting Raffles, arrives at the estate. As people begin to retire for the evening Raffles notices the maid turning off the alarm and letting a burglar in. The robber steals Lady Melrose's necklace, but Raffles takes the necklace away. The thief cannot see Raffles's face but notices the watch around his wrist. After the robbery is discovered Lady Melrose offers a thousand pounds reward. The robber is captured, but as he stands there surrounded by the people at the estate he recognizes Raffles's watch. When the necklace is not discovered, Inspector Mackenzie purposely releases the thief and has him followed. The thief, of course, goes to Raffles's house to get the necklace. Raffles has by then given the necklace to Bunny to get the reward. The inspector has Raffles cornered. After admitting that he was indeed "The Amateur Cracksman" who had left the calling cards, Raffles escapes using a detective's coat as his disguise. At the conclusion of the film Raffles gives himself up.

It is easy to see this movie, as the *New York Times*'s film critic did, as a "tribute to burglary," a playing off of the Robin Hood

myth or the robber as folk-hero myth, that had developed in postwar
America of the twenties and thirties. Indeed, some of that myth is in
the film. The thief decides to quit for love. He only engages in the
one additional theft that will prove to be his undoing to help out a
friend in trouble. These melodramatic, clichéd plot elements set
alongside the clichéd character of a gentleman-thief with a heart of
gold do pander to the American myth. Yet underneath this pander-
ing it is possible to see in *Raffles* the raising of a serious social
question: How should money be parceled out. There is tremendous
inequality in the society in this film. Of course the inequality of
money is not a theme that is pursued, yet money is the motivating
factor for the characters in the film, and this factor—looming larger
even than love—is at the center of the plot. The implicit question
is: Why should money be so important? The obvious answer—
greed—is dismissed in Raffles's case in favor of a more complex
phenomenon: the recognition that some people who have more than
enough money should be forced to give some of their money to
those who need it. Stated baldly, this theme will, in fact, later
emerge in *The Best Years of Our Lives*. In *Raffles* it is hidden, barely
visible under the veneer of light entertainment and good-natured
fun which the audience expected.

Even though *Raffles* was meant to be seen as pure entertainment,
the film was still an occasion for *Times's* critic Frank S. Nugent to
marvel at the precision with which Goldwyn made a movie. Nugent
reproduced a note prefacing the script: "As the entire action of the
picture happens within a couple of days in London, during the
cricket season, there cannot be any fog as there has always been in
previous 'Raffles' pictures. London fogs, however bad, do not
happen in the Summer, and cricket doesn't happen in the Winter."
This attention to exact detail, even in an entertainment film, is
illustrative of Goldwyn's consistently high standards, his refusal to
make a cheap film for popular consumption at bargain prices. "He's
a stickler for form, even when the form is . . . formular. . . ." As he
had all his professional life, Goldwyn continued to make entertainments for the mass audience which would charm them, thrill them,
please them—and possibly, in other films to which this public would
go to because of the Goldwyn name, he would do all these plus give
them culture, make them think, and educate them.

Ball of Fire (1941)

Goldwyn's limited encounter with screwball comedies that had
started with *Woman Chases Man* concluded with *Ball of Fire*, his

second and final attempt in the genre. This film was based on a story by Billy Wilder. (Wilder gained a good deal of experience during the film; he observed director Howard Hawks at work and then went on to direct his own films.) Goldwyn bought it as a comedy for Gary Cooper.

The story in the movie involves a group of seven professors who together are working on an encyclopedia. Professor Bertram Potts is assigned to write about "slang" and, having led a somewhat sheltered life, decides to gather information about "slang" on a firsthand basis. In his pursuit of knowledge he unknowingly gets into trouble with the police, and that trouble leads him to a stripper named Sugarpuss O'Shea, whom he knew from a previous attempt to find out about slang. Sugarpuss, in trouble with a ganster named Joe Lilac, wants to hide out and decides that she will accept the professor's invitation to visit him. She meets the entire group and they invite her to stay with them so that they may study her quaint slang. Her humor, her evening conga lessons, and her knowledge of every aspect of slang, make all the professors, including Potts, find her attractive, and their normal life is disrupted, to their immense enjoyment. When Lilac's henchmen catch up to her and tell her she has to leave to marry Lilac, she realizes that she is in love with Potts. Potts, wishing to aid her, tells her he will drive her to New Jersey. Once there the professors are taken prisoner by Lilac's men until Sugarpuss marries the gangster. But the professors outwit the gangsters and have them captured just as the police come in. Sugarpuss and Potts are reunited.

Time magazine's critic captured best the spirit of the film: *Ball of Fire*, their critic wrote, "is saturated with some of the juiciest, wackiest, solid American slang ever recorded on celluloid. The plot is not as fresh as its idea, but the picture will do until its producer . . . wins his own lifelong race with the English language."[15] The critic noted the self-mockery and the sassiness. If Cooper seemed strangely cast as a shy, scholarly professor, not many complained about the fact. Instead the film stands as a screwball comedy with the most precise and most varied use of American slang to achieve its humor.

They Got Me Covered (1943)

Goldwyn, like every other filmmaker, faced a number of questions directly raised by the onset of war. One practical problem was replacing the numerous actors, actresses, writers, technicians, directors, and other screen personnel who volunteered to fight. As a

patriotric American Goldwyn wanted to infuse his films with a sense
of the war. But that was the problem. As Richard Griffith puts it,
"The onset of World War II faced screen writers with a problem.
Films from now on must be war-related to some degree, but in what
degree? No one could forsee the shape and content of the experience
to come and in the mean time there was no guidepost at hand but
the hoary model of World War I, whose melodramatic films had
centered around Hunnish *Schrechlichkeit,* and whose plots, by
endless repetition through the intervening years, had become as
familiar and as unexciting as the sun at noon. Still, there was
nothing for it for the time being but to dress the old stories in Nazi
and Japanese uniforms." ·

That was precisely the solution Goldwyn hit upon. He reread a
property that he already owned, "Washington Melodrama," written
by Leonard Spigelgass and Leonard Q. Ross, and found it useful.
"It's cliches had become almost gags." Goldwyn's ability with broad
comedy was almost as weak as his musical abilities, however.

Bob Hope, who made films generally with Paramount, was hired
to star in the film along with Dorothy Lamour, Hope's co-star in
many of his "Road" pictures. Goldwyn saw in Hope the kind of
wise-cracking comic who would bring desperately needed laughs to
film audiences. To keep the Road team almost complete, Goldwyn
hired David Butler, the director of *Road to Morocco,* to direct the
film. The movie, like a screwball comedy, had a fast-paced plot and
witty dialogue. *They Got Me Covered* tells the story of not-so-ace
reporter Robert Kittredge. Kittredge has been assigned as a foreign
correspondent to Moscow but has missed the story of the German
invasion (he saw the soldiers and thought he was witnessing a
parade). After this, Kittredge's boss, Norman Mason, fires him.
Dejected, and vowing to return, Kittredge travels to Washington to
see Christina Hill, an ex-girl friend. He is not there only for romance
though; Christina runs the Washington bureau of Amalgamated
News. Christina shares her apartment with a number of other
women in apartment-short Washington and, despite some skepti-
cism, is clearly in love with Kittredge.

While in Washington hoping to prove his capabilities as a
newsman, Kittredge is approached by Gregory Vanescu, a spy.
Vanescu offers to sell Kittredge important information about a den
of spies operating in the nation's capital. Kittredge gets the money,
$5,000, from Christina and agrees. They arrange to meet, but at the
last moment Vanescu is frightened when some of the spies appear.

Vanescu gets word to Kittredge to have a stenographer sent to a prearranged meeting place so that Vanescu can dictate what he knows. Christina sends Sally, one of her roommates (who has a very big, jealous boy friend), to take the dictation. Sally does meet Vanescu and he tells her all, but as she rushes back to tell Christina and Kittredge, she is kidnapped by the spies who had been following Vanescu. The leader of the spy network, Otto Fauscheim (played by Otto Preminger) plan to have Kittredge appear a national fool.

Using a beautiful woman named Margo Vanescu as bait to trick Kittredge into thinking he will learn the facts about the spies and Sally's whereabouts, he goes with this woman but is drugged by her. He wakes up in a bed in Niagara Falls and is married to a pretty blonde striptease artist, known in the trade as Gloria the Glow Girl. He rushes from his bed and looks out the window where photographers, who have been notified of his marriage, take his picture, which appears on front pages throughout the country.

Kittredge returns to Washington to convince Christina that he loves her, that his "marriage" was a plot against him, and to convince Sally's angry boy friend that she will be found. Christina does believe him because she knows a fact about him: he does not like blondes. Gloria, the stripper, finding out the reason behind what she believed to be no more than a harmless prank, decides to reveal the truth, but before she can she is murdered on stage. Kittredge examines her dressing room and he finds information there leading him to a beauty salon in Washington which is, in fact, the spy network's headquarters. He tells Christina where he is and, disguised as a woman, he enters the salon. He is discovered and chased throughout. Pretending to be a dummy he hears the full plans. Christina meanwhile has entered the salon pretending to be a customer, and with her roomates' help discovers the truth. She calls the F.B.I., whose agents enter and round up all the spies. Sally is found safe, Kittredge and Christina plan to marry, Kittredge wins a prize and gets his job back.

The film is packed with Hope witticisms. In fact, Hope is so central to the film, that it is on him that the entire film rests, an unusual case for a Goldwyn film in general but *not* for his entertainment films which failed in part because of their overreliance on the screen character of a leading star, whether Cantor or Danny Kaye or Hope. *Newsweek*'s critic expressed the public as well as critics' opinion most clearly: "*They Got Me Covered* will be welcomed by Hope's fans, but it falls short of the comedian's best. . . . The letdown apparently was in the writing department. . . . Hope's comic genius springs eternal with only intermittent leverage from a script that strains for the irresponsible idiocy of his recent vehicles. Of even less help is the casting of Dorothy Lamour in a role that requires the erstwhile 'Alonma of the South Seas' to talk a lot more than usual and wear twice as much—a self-defeating enterprise whatever way you look at it." [16]

The film did make money, however, and Goldwyn was convinced by the profits that Hope's enormous following and tremendous comic talents would turn another Goldwyn film into a comic masterpiece. It was not to be however. Hope did make one more film for Goldwyn, *The Princess and the Pirate* (1944), a costume drama about the characters in the title. The writing in this film was so weak, the situations so remote from the urban, contemporary settings in which Hope worked so well, or the historical settings he could manipulate (such as the Old West), or the foreign locales which the Road pictures featured, that Hope looked simply out of place. After this debacle Hope and Goldwyn parted company.

In retrospect, while *The Princess and the Pirate* can be dismissed as a misfire, *They Got Me Covered* stands as symbolic of the type of wartime comedies that audiences found attractive. It is perhaps the best example of that particular type.

Danny Kaye Movies

Samuel Goldwyn made a special effort to see Danny Kaye perform because of all the reports he was receiving about the young Borschtbelt trained comedian who was such a success in the Broadway play *Lady in the Dark*. Goldwyn went to see the show, recognized Kaye's talents (Goldwyn laughed; therefore, Goldwyn assumed, movie audiences would laugh as well), but immediately recognized the problem Kaye would have in becoming acceptable as a film star: his looks. Goldwyn thought Kaye to be unphotogenic, but changed his mind after observing further performances and noting the attachment audiences had. Goldwyn signed the comedian, already famous for the "scat" (songs that sound like jazz music but that contain syllables that make no sense) written by his wife Sylvia Fine. Goldwyn then returned to Hollywood, looking for a story that would suit Kaye's peculiar abilities.

After dismissing numerous attempts Goldwyn settled on a new version of the Eddie Cantor success *Whoopee!* The screenplay was supplemented with Sylvia Fine's material. Goldwyn then brought

Kaye to Hollywood for a screen test. To Goldwyn's mind the results of that and other tests was disastrous. Kaye's face, made angular by its thinness, was not the face of a comic but a villain. Goldwyn pondered the problem, unable for a long while to come up with a solution. Finally, as he watched, he hit upon the answer: Kaye's hair was to be dyed blond. On screen this changed his appearance, making him, to Goldwyn, cheerful. The plot in *Up in Arms* set the standard for future Kaye fare.

The story revolves around one Danny Weems, who is a hypochiondriac. Danny is so worried about being sick that he wants to be near his doctors constantly. This desire makes him take a job operating an elevator in a medical center. The army, unimpressed with his self-diagnosed maladies, drafts both him and his roommate. Both of their girl friends also go into the service. His roommate, Joe Nelson, is, in fact, loved by Danny's girl friend, Mary Morgan. It is Mary's friend Virginia Merrill, who likes Danny. After they have been trained, they are about to be sent to the South Pacific.

On board waiting to leave, the girls, who have left the nurses regiment to which they belong, come to see them. Because of Danny's mistake, the girls are on board the ship as it leaves the harbor. Unlike Virginia, who, as a nurse, can lie about her presence on board, Mary has no useful excuse. To prevent Mary's discovery, Danny tries a variety of tactics so that Colonel Ashley, the commanding officer on the ship, will not find out about her. When she is finally discovered Danny assumes responsibility. After the ship arrives in the South Pacific Danny, as expected, is placed under arrest and put in a small guardhouse near the camp.

During a Japanese raid, the Japanese overrun the small guardhouse and capture Danny. Disguising himself Danny fools them and eventually he leads them to be captured. This act turns him into a hero.

Critics loved the movie. Bosley Crowther of the *New York Times* thought the film needed "more of a story" but he too was seduced by Kaye's charms. He asked rhetorically, after expounding on Kaye's comedic talents (and Dinah Shore's singing), "what more could a person need to be entertained?"[17] *Time* admired Kaye as well, and claimed that his "mimicry, patter and general daftness are as deft as a surgeon's incision."[18] Audiences and critics both overlooked the silliness of the story, instead accepting as admirable moviemaking the sheer comic entertainment provided by the specialty numbers such as "Melody in F" which was to become Kaye's trademark. This ability to accept second-rate material provided the star was sufficiently good—an ability exhibited by an earlier generation who watched the six Eddie Cantor films—probably hurt Goldwyn more than it helped, because a failure, or a series of failures, with his entertainment films would have forced him to confront their essential weaknesses: the lack of a story line which was coherent and important (instead of the trivial ones he had) and the inability to unite the disparate elements of his entertainment films—the music, comedy, and dances—with the story. His commercial successes simply reenforced in his mind the idea that he was doing the genre right and it was not until late in his life that he came to realize that it was precisely the films which were commercially successful (in most cases) which he was unable to make aesthetic successes. Kaye went on after *Up in Arms* to make *Wonder Man* (1945) and *The Kid From Brooklyn* (1946) (an extremely financially successful film about a milk truck driver who becomes a great boxer) and *A Song is Born* (1948), a remake of *Ball of Fire*, besides his two important films for Goldwyn: *The Secret Life of Walter Mitty* (1947) and *Hans Christian Andersen* (1952).

The Secret Life of Walter Mitty (1947)

Walter Mitty is, perhaps, the definitive James Thurber character, and, in print at least, a character reflecting American males' lives with a piercing insightfulness. Mitty is a man whose masculinity has been taken from him, who struggles with his humdrum life of quiet desperation by daydreaming, by placing himself in exciting, dangerous situations, meaningful because the secure, protected, sanitized world Mitty really inhabits no longer suffices. That real world inhabited by the literary Mitty was one marked by a shrew for a wife and an inability to understand or use the gadgets of modern life.

The ease with which American men in particular could identify with Walter Mitty could be seen in the number and variety of responses Thurber received from readers of the story when it appeared in *The New Yorker* on March 18, 1939.

Sam Goldwyn never read the Thurber story. Nevertheless, on the basis of a synopsis, Goldwyn decided to buy the story in 1944 for $15,000. After Danny Kaye's 1946 film *The Kid From Brooklyn* had become an enormous success, Goldwyn wished to film his star quickly in another suitable movie and decided upon Thurber's story.

Goldwyn, however, had slightly miscalculated. After listening to the synopsis, Goldwyn had come to a false conclusion that the story was essentially comic and light, and, as such, made suitable fare for the joking and singing that Danny Kaye fans wished to see. What Goldwyn missed was the contradiction between the meek, henpecked Mitty and the bouncy, cheerful, energetic Kaye. One would have to be sacrificed.

At first Goldwyn was sure about the dream sequence in which Mitty fantasizes about his masculinity. Goldwyn was sure they formed an important part of the film. At his studio, however, there were those who thought the character too parochial, too much a *New Yorker* character and too little a type of character associated with Danny Kaye. Kaye himself, and his wife Sylvia Fine, were concerned that the Mitty character was too restrictive for the Kaye screen persona. When they mentioned this to Goldwyn, the producer agreed. He, too, was interested in making a popular movie for the entire country, not one which appealed to a select few.

When Goldwyn confronted Ken Englund, the scriptwriter, England, noting that the original Thurber piece had been reprinted in *Reader's Digest,* argued for the universal appeal of Thurber's original conception. Thurber himself noted in the August 4, 1947, issue of *Life* that if Danny Kaye starred in it, "The Secret Life of Walter Mitty" would be transformed into "The Public Life of Danny Kaye."

Goldwyn, concerned about following up on Kaye's success but sympathetic to the literary intentions of Thurber, tried for a compromise. The Mitty character's name was retained as were some general characteristics—such as fantasizing—but the character became more like Danny Kaye's previous screen characters than James Thurber's literary creature.

After a script was completed in November, 1945, even prior to the release of *The Kid From Brooklyn,* Goldwyn was considering Kaye as Walter Mitty. Goldwyn met with Thurber about the script, and Thurber was incensed by the humorous but typical Danny Kaye routines, by the change from Mitty having a nagging wife to having a nagging mother, by Sylvia Fine's "patter" songs, and by a script Thurber judged too melodramatic.

Goldwyn decided to cancel the film, and then retracted that decision. He had Ken Englund work with Thurber on the script. Specifically, Goldwyn noted the last sixty pages of the script were weak and so he wanted more action. When Thurber read the revision he was upset about the violence; he had pictured his story as simply charming and humorous. Thurber determined to remove what he considered to be excessive reliance on physical force. Almost all of his suggestions were rejected. Thurber then publicly disclaimed an association with the film. The August 18, 1947, issue of *Life* (the film had been released earlier that week) carried two letters, an exchange between producer and author. Goldwyn, in soft language, tried to suggest what Thurber had contributed to the movie. Thurber, more acerbic, ended a detailed account of his participation by writing "Sorry, Walter, sorry for Everything."

The story of Goldwyn's Walter Mitty is as follows: Walter Mitty is a meek son and employee. His mother reminds him of endless errands she wants him to perform for her and for his boss, Bruce Pierce, who towers over him even while stealing his excellent business ideas. Mitty's mother has arranged a marriage for Walter with a young woman with interests much different from his, including an overriding concern for the comfort of her dog. To escape this binding world in which he lives Walter dreams while he drives, while he walks, or while he is supposed to be working.

James Thurber's timid dreamer finds himself in a tight spot: Danny Kaye in The Secret Life of Walter Mitty.

Altogether the film has eight dream sequences scattered through the movie. In these sequences Walter is always daring and always sees a beautiful blonde. In various sequences Walter sees himself as an eminent surgeon, a Mississippi gambler, a gunfighter, and a gallant RAF Wing Commander, among others.

One day on the train a woman sits down beside Walter. He is astonished to discover that she is the blonde woman from out of his daydreams. The woman, Rosalind Van Hoorn (Virginia Mayo), requests that Walter help her escape a man who is following her. Mitty helps her twice, but after the dead body of her friend is discovered in a cab, Walter wants to go to work. Walter eventually is told her story. Her uncle holds valuable jewels which international jewel thieves are attempting to steal. For helping Rosalind, Walter is almost thrown out the window by an attacker. The man Rosalind thought to be her uncle turns out not to be. Confused by all the turmoil in his life Walter tries to explain the situation to his mother and fiancée. Convinced by his tale that he is crazy the two women decide to take him to a psychiatrist. When Walter meets the psychiatrist, Dr. Hollingshead (Boris Karloff), he is startled: Hollingshead is the man who attempted to kill him. Eventually the phony doctor convinces Mitty that all his experiences were imagined. Walter finally accepts this explanation and plans are made for the wedding. At the wedding Walter reaches into his pocket and feels something Rosalind gave him. He suddenly realizes that his experiences were true and the psychiatrist is part of the group of jewel thieves. Walter rushes away before the wedding is completed and goes to Rosalind's home. There he frees the captured Rosalind and rounds up the entire ring of thieves. He and Rosalind plan to wed, and at work he confronts his boss and, astounded at the change, his boss gives him a raise.

Critics by and large liked the film, seeing it as it was meant to be seen: as a vehicle for Danny Kaye's talents but not as a faithful translation of a short story. Goldwyn conceived of the film as a comedy, but not of the sort offered in the wistful story. The comedy in the film was meant to be broader, with more emphasis on the physical than the intellectual. Goldwyn's conception of comedy often was translated as putting an inept and bumbling hero into a situation of great danger. The hero, winning a beautiful woman also in danger who often turns to him for help, triumphs over the evil machinations of the villains. This plot outline was useful in such other films as the two Bob Hope did for Goldwyn: *The Princess and the Pirate* (1944) and *They Got Me Covered* (1943), and was built upon the earlier successes of the Eddie Cantor films. Audiences were certainly delighted with this mix of exaggerated action, low drama, and physical comedy, and they showed their delight over and over again through ticket purchases.

Hans Christian Andersen (1952)

As in the case of so many of the musicals which Goldwyn produced, *Hans Christian Andersen* had been in Goldwyn's mind as a potential film for many years before the actual film was completed. Originally, the project was intended to star Gary Cooper, to be directed by William Wyler, and to be completed in the late 1930s. Goldwyn, however, never received a satisfactory script.

By the mid-1940s along with Danny Kaye's exploding popularity came a search for films for Kaye to star in. *The Secret Life of Walter Mitty* was one of these films and *Hans Christian Andersen* another. Despite the star and the idea, because of script problems it still took over five years to complete the film. In all Goldwyn read through a total of sixteen screenplays, settling at last on that written by Moss Hart (the famous comedic playwright and collaborator with George S. Kaufman on numerous Broadway hits). Perhaps even more than in his dramatic films Goldwyn was so anxious to succeed in his musical films that he spent lavishly, almost ridiculously. All in all *Hans Christian Andersen* cost over four million dollars. Of this sum over $14,000 was spent on shoes, $400,000 on one seventeen-minute ballet sequence, and $175,000 (then a very high salary) paid for Kaye's service. The only casting problem occurred when Moira Shearer, a well-known British ballerina, became pregnant and had to withdraw from the film. Her place was taken by Renée Jeanmaire.

Moss Hart's script, under Goldwyn's careful watch, cannot be considered a faithful rendition of Andersen's life, a fact which did not go unnoticed in Denmark and was later to receive much protest. Evidently Goldwyn conceived of the film's possibilities not as just a musical, not as just a biography, and not as just a film for Danny Kaye. He was enchanted by the notion of making a fairy tale about the world's most famous fairy-tale creator. Thus much of the movie has an aura of fantasy about it, an aura that Goldwyn very much intended for there to be. The opening credits of the film disclaim any notion that the movie presents or intends to present an accurate retelling of Hans Christian Andersen's life.

The story told in the movie does, in fact, sound like a fairy tale.

Hans Christian Andersen lives in the town of Odense. There he owns a shoe-repair shop but spends much of his time enchanting the school children of the town with tales which he has invented. Because the children listen to Hans rather than attend school, the schoolmaster is angered and convinces the leaders of the town that Hans is having a detrimental effect on the children's education. Hans is asked to leave. Pondering his fate with his young helper Peter, Hans kiddingly suggests he will go to Copenhagen. Peter tells him he should, and Hans decides that he will head for that city which has mythic proportions to him. He leaves and Peter later follows him. They meet on the road and together journey to Copenhagen.

Once they are settled in the city, Hans again opens a cobbler's shop but soon gets into trouble with the law and is arrested. Peter, seeking to avoid the police, hides out at the Royal Theater where the ballet company is rehearsing. He sees the prima ballerina arguing with the ballet director. She complains that she needs a cobbler. Seizing the moment, Peter rushes out and says he knows where a cobbler can be found at that hour: in jail. Hans is then bailed out of jail and rushed over to the theater to fix the ballet shoes.

Hans does his best, but is distracted by the beauty of Doro, the ballerina. When he sees Doro arguing violently with Neils, the director, he attempts to come to her aid but is ordered to leave and not to return during any rehearsal. Hans is not aware that Doro and Neils are husband and wife, happily married, and that their arguments remain only within the confines of their professional work. Returning home Hans realizes that he is in love with Doro and composes a fairy tale entitled "The Little Mermaid," which is a thinly disguised plea to her to get away from the mean Neils and be with him. Through Peter's carelessness and the wind, Doro sees a copy of the fairy tale, but she misinterprets it to be the basis of a ballet. Peter ashamedly tells Hans that the ballerina has the tale, and Hans, thinking he will have won her when she reads it goes to see her. By the time he arrives, the ballet troupe has disappeared, gone on a tour. He thinks of her as he continues as a cobbler. He also continues to tell his stories to any children he meets. One day he sees a boy whose head is practically bald. The saddened boy is cheered up considerably when Hans tells him a tale about "The Ugly Duckling." The boy tells his father who is a newspaper publisher and the publisher requests Hans's permission to reprint the tale. Hans gratefully accepts. The story is well-received and Hans achieves a good deal of fame. Just as the fame comes, the ballet troupe returns to town with their new ballet "The Little Mermaid." Hans goes to the ballet and demands to be allowed to present Doro a special pair of shoes he has made. Neils refuses to let him see her, and when Hans does not leave quietly Neils locks him in a closet. Hans overhears the entire ballet and imagines each of the scenes. On the morning after the ballet, Doro is worried about Hans because he did not attend the performance. It is then that she learns of his confrontation with her husband. The ballerina sends a message requesting to see Hans. When he arrives Doro immediately understands that he is in love with her. She tells him that she and Neils are very happily married. Distraught, Hans decides to return to his home town. when he arrives back in Odense he is greeted as a famous man and everyone, adults as well as children, are delighted by his stories.

Reaction was varied. The Danes were angry at what they saw as an insult to the memory of their most famous writer. Goldwyn's planned Copenhagen world premiere seemed doomed until the world wide success of Frank Loesser's song "Wonderful Copenhagen" resulted in a travel boom for Denmark. Goldwyn was then allowed his cherished premiere.

The critics had mixed opinions. All of them agreed that the film depended too much on Danny Kaye in what, for him, was clearly a restrained performance. Some liked this change from the effervescent, overactive personna he had developed, but Hollis Alpert, writing in *Saturday Review*, sums up the reason for the movie's failure:

"Kaye . . . has been kept under such restraint that his performance has all the zest of a glass of beer gone flat. Without any clowning to do, Danny Kaye is simply not very interesting, and it's hard to get worked up over his encounter with a ballet dancer in Copenhagen and his rather foolish mooning over her."[19] Bosley Crowther of the *New York Times* notices this same failure but blamed Moss Hart for not creating a character magnetic enough for Kaye's particular talents.[20] Whether Kaye, Hart, or Goldwyn are to blame, *Hans Christian Andersen* cannot be considered a success, and once more for Goldwyn a musical he thought would be groundbreaking turned out flat. This, of course, is only in a critical sense. Commercially, the film made six million dollars, making it Goldwyn's third most successful film in his entire career (after *The*

Best Years of Our Lives and *Guys and Dolls*). Satisfied as Goldwyn was with this kind of success, it was not enough for him, and the elusive creation known as the musical was still the cinematic form he had not conquered; Goldwyn, being Goldwyn, refused to give up.

Guys and Dolls (1955)

Goldwyn spent one million dollars in cash to acquire rights to film *Guys and Dolls*, a price that was at that time the largest ever paid for one property. *Guys and Dolls* had already established itself as a Broadway hit and that, to Goldwyn, was the insurance he had always sought before filming. In addition, the play was based on a story by Damon Runyon. Runyon was not, perhaps, a writer accepted in elite writing circles, but he was certainly a talented writer of specialized humor.

In the tradition of hiring popular actors, Goldwyn chose Marlon Brando and Jean Simmons. The choice seemed odd because neither one of them could sing or dance yet were to star in what was to be an elaborate musical. Goldwyn also chose the popular Frank Sinatra to play Nathan Detroit, a character portrayed by Sam Levene in the stage play. Again this was a surprise because Levene had received such excellent critical notices.

By the time of its completion the film cost $5.5 million to produce, a staggering sum for a mid 1950s film, when television was threatening the very existence of film by robbing the theater of viewers, and when producers were careful about spending their money. In an era of frugality and conservatism (taking no chances on new stars or unusual themes) Goldwyn, once more in his life, defied Hollywood "wisdom."

As in many of the Goldwyn musicals the story is flimsy. The musical stories were meant to be threads between songs and production numbers. In the musicals the audience was dazzled by costumes, singing, and dancing—not by plot and dialogue. Because of this the emphasis is musical entertainment.

Guys and Dolls is set in the Runyonesque world of gamblers, shady characters (all of whom are tagged with unusual nicknames, such as Harry the Horse, Nicely-Nicely Johnson, and Angie the Ox), and women capable of redeeming these underworld types. Instead of violence, Runyon's underworld is filled with laughter and music.

Sky Masterson (Brando), a successful gambler, falls in love with Sarah Brown (Jean Simmons) who runs the Save-a-Soul mission on

Broadway. Another gambler, Nathan Detroit, who controls the
longest-running crap game in history, is always in need of money to
rent space for any available place to keep his gambling in motion.
Nathan has been engaged for fourteen years to Miss Adelaide
(Vivian Blaine), who is in the chorus line of a cheap entertainment
joint. The two are constantly battling over the nature of their
relationship, especially its future.

Nathan, desperately in need of money, makes a thousand-dollar
bet with Sky that Masterson cannot get the Puritanical Sarah to
accompany him on a trip to Havana. Sky, eager to win his bet,
knows Sarah wants to save the souls of Sky's numerous gambling
friends and so he promises her that in return for her company on the
trip he, in turn, will bring a dozen of "the devil's first-string troops"
to the mission for her to save. She considers the proposal and finally
accepts it. After the trip, Sky, having fallen in love with Sarah, does
not want Nathan and his gambling buddies to draw incorrect
conclusions about any amourous nature of the trip so he denies he
was successful in getting Sarah to go, thereby losing his bet. To
keep his word to Sarah he rounds up twelve of his friends and
delivers them to her mission. The movie concludes with Nathan and
Miss Adelaide and Sky and Sarah getting married in Times Square.

The film was moderately successful monetarily, but less so
artistically. Goldwyn did make his money back plus a few million
dollars in profit. But to the careful observer the film had a Goldwyn
touch but not a Goldwyn grip. Goldwyn was simply unable to
maintain as completely as he had done in the past the sorts of
control over every aspect of production that had marked all his
efforts.

Critical reaction was one of muted enthusiasm. The performances
were generally liked but approval was not overwhelming. Stephen
Sondheim in *Films in Review* noted an interesting flaw: "Samuel
Goldwyn, Joseph Mankiewicz and Mr. Smith [Oliver Smith, who
created the sets] apparently couldn't make up their mind whether
the scenery should be realistic or stylized. As a result, they have the
disadavantages of both, and those disadvantages work against the
very special nature of Runyonesque story-telling. . . ."[21] Goldwyn,
of course, often was susceptible to the same charge, that of mixing
the real and the fantastical. Certainly in *Walter Mitty*, in almost all
his musical and comedy entertainments, Goldwyn had not been
satisfied with presenting a film clearly in one genre. He thought
audiences appreciated the mix and thought they were getting more

for their money if adventure was mixed with comedy, or political adventure with comedy, or realistic drama with musical. If these types did not always mesh well that was an aesthetic fault in a movie designed for popular entertainment and as such not fatal.

Guys and Dolls, even as popular entertainment, failed to provide really memorable scenes with the possible exceptions of the twelve men in the mission and the "Luck Be A Lady" dance sequence, but certainly even including these, there were no scenes comparable to Dana Andrews sitting in the airplane cockpit in *The Best Years of Our Lives* or Barbara Stanwyck standing in the rain watching her daughter's wedding, in the remake of *Stella Dallas* (1937).

Porgy and Bess (1959)

Three years after *Guys and Dolls* Goldwyn, curiously, again chose for his final production a musical, not the area of his notable achievement. It is possible of course that he recognized this, and that right up until the very end of his career he was trying to produce a musical which would be as popular and as powerful as his dramas.

Haunted by *The Goldwyn Follies* and other critical failures, by his own sense of failure in the production of musicals, Goldwyn, who had conquered other areas of filmmaking, chose to concentrate his last efforts not on redoing what he had already been praised for but in continuing to perfect his talent, deliberately to confront his area of greatest weakness, by attempting to film America's most outstanding original contribution to music drama.

If his aim was to wed the success of his serious dramas, most especially *The Best Years of Our Lives,* with the popularity of the musical form, it is easy to see why he chose to film *Porgy and Bess:* this was one musical with a serious social message, or at least as far as Goldwyn saw it. The use of black Americans so exclusively in a film was unique for Goldwyn—or for most Hollywood producers up to that time.

The place of blacks in American culture was of course widely debated. Goldwyn's film was made, after all, only five years after the landmark 1954 decision by the Supreme Court outlawing segregation. In the case of *Porgy and Bess,* however, such vital sociological elements to the discussion of the film were irrelevant to Goldwyn. He, in fact, had always enjoyed the folk opera by DuBose Heyward. Goldwyn had seen it on stage in 1935 and from that moment had loved it. For Goldwyn the libretto by Heyward, when

Goldwyn's last musical spectacles: (top) Frank Sinatra (center) in the "Luck Be A Lady" number from Guys and Dolls; *(bottom) Sidney Poitier and Dorothy Dandridge (center) during a happy moment in* Porgy and Bess.

combined with George Gershwin's incomparable musical composi-
tions, made *Porgy and Bess* the superlative American musical.
Goldwyn especially admired Gershwin (fondly keeping an auto-
graphed portrait of the composer in his office) and meant *Porgy and
Bess* in part as a tribute to Gershwin's genius. Finally, Goldwyn
knew how expansive the screen was in comparison to the stage and
was able to imagine how effective a screen adaptation could be.

It took Goldwyn eleven years to acquire the rights to *Porgy and
Bess*. The legal difficulties of dealing with the estates of Heyward
and Gershwin were overcome only to be followed by a bidding war
between Goldwyn and the other major studio heads. Finally Goldwyn offered $650,000 in cash plus ten percent of the gross receipts
(producers almost never offered a percentage of the gross receipts,
instead using a fixed percentage of the net receipts which were
susceptible to a considerable amount of manipulation).

Already owning a property that he considered to be as well-done
as possible, Goldwyn had his scriptwriter N. Richard Nash keep the
original virtually intact. Rouben Mamoulian (famous for his work in
developing sound films into genuine art, and who had directed for
Goldwyn before in *We Live Again*) was hired as director.

Soon after the script and director were set, Goldwyn's fortunes
reversed; the film ran into innumerable difficulties, certainly enough
to have stopped most producers let alone one a decade beyond the
usual retirement age. Goldwyn immediately ran into opposition
from black civil rights groups, anxious about a story in which blacks
were presented as sly, vicious, and brutal. The story seemed to black
leaders to be full of racial stereotypes. The Council for the Improvement of Negro Theater Arts took out a double-page ad. Almena
Lomax, author of the ad, expressed the opinion of the Council that
no film of *Porgy and Bess* could be done tastefully because of the
nature of the material itself. The ad ran: "Dorothy and DuBose
Heyward used the race situation in the South to write a lot of
allegories in which Negroes were violent or gentle, humble or
conniving. . . . But it never occurred to them that the Negro was not
innately any of this, and that he was just like anybody else and that
this was a human being's way of reacting to the dehumanizing
pressure of a master race."[22]

Castigating Goldwyn for his failure to hire blacks at his studio,
the ad also declared that it would be wrong for any black performers
to participate in the production of *Porgy and Bess*. Because of the
various black groups' dissapproval, there was a great deal of

difficulty in casting the film. For his part, Goldwyn was shocked at the views expressed by these groups. Goldwyn found in the story some of his familiar themes which, he believed, were suppotive of minority rights, the fight against injustice, and the staggering effects poverty has upon the human being struggling for personal fulfillment. Goldwyn noted that black performers had often starred in productions of the folk opera. Seeking to assuage the black community, Goldwyn gave $1,000 to the local NAACP, a gift which was met with accusations of using money to gain acceptance. Those black actors and actresses who had signed to be in the film appeared at press conferences only to be accused of being "Uncle Toms."

The turning point in the casting of the film came about when Sidney Poitier agreed to be in the film, contingent upon a satisfactory personal meeting with Goldwyn. The meeting was held and Poitier was convinced. After Poitier's signing, Pearl Bailey and Dorothy Dandridge also signed, and most black groups gave up resisting the making of the film.

Goldwyn assembled the remainder of his production team. He brought in Andre Previn to do the music and used Hollywood's second biggest sound stage to recreate Catfish Row, the Charleston setting of the film. To build this magnificent set, Goldwyn spent two million dollars.

The film finally seemed ready to begin. The first dress rehearsal was scheduled for July 3, but just before dawn on that morning a suspicious fire broke out on the stage, destroying it entirely. Goldwyn, at age seventy-five, did not look at the ruins. He was told it would take two months and two and a half million dollars to replace the sets. That afternoon he ordered work to begin again.

Rouben Mamoulian was another casualty of the fire. The director was having difficulties with the cast and with Goldwyn. Goldwyn replaced him with Otto Preminger, who had just finished directing the all-black film *Carmen Jones*. Preminger, unlike Wyler and Mamoulian, who had loud and direct confrontations with Goldwyn, chose to assert his directorial authority in a novel way: he shot very few extra scenes. In effect, he was editing as he was shooting and so Goldwyn, with little extra footage to manipulate, was left angry but unable to alter much. Goldwyn was reluctant to fire a second director in a film already so troubled.

The story of *Porgy and Bess* is, of course, subordinate to the musical elements of the film. The movie begins with the mean Crown beating a gambler to death. Crown desires Bess and eventually rapes her. Porgy, a beggar who is crippled, loves Bess too despite her immoral past. These and other characters on Catfish Row including the corruptive drug-addict Sportin' Life live out their daily lives throughout the movie up to the climatic hurricane.

The themes developed in the film are familiar ones. Porgy and Bess's love is doomed because of their surroundings; Bess's desire to be free of the Catfish Row life is doomed; in short, the black characters in *Porgy and Bess* are trapped in a violent world they did not create and from which they cannot escape. Goldwyn avoided the central question of white guilt, satisfied that he had made a realistic portrayal of the devastation racial hatred can have.

Critics were generally extremely favorable. Bosley Crowther in the *New York Times* ended his review with these words: "For the most part, this is a stunning, exciting and moving film, packed with human emotions and cheerful and mournful melodies. It bids fair to be as much a classic on the screen as it is on the stage."[23]

The moviegoing public was not as kind as the critics. They simply did not like the film; their reaction deeply disappointed Goldwyn.

Porgy and Bess turned out to be Goldwyn's last chance to make a musical as comparably successful in popular entertainment as *The Best Years of Our Lives* had been in serious drama. It must have bothered him terribly that he failed.

7

Americana

America

AN ARTIST'S PRODUCTS ARE inevitably grounded in the artist's experiences, as well as the application of imagination to those experiences. One of the most crucial experiences for Goldwyn involved his journey to America. Interestingly and significantly, he did not make films about immigrants because, at bottom he thought of himself as an American born by accident in another country.

When Samuel Goldwyn first came to America in 1896 he was a boy in search of a dream. Over a half century later, when his phenomenal producing career ended with his retirement in 1959, he was wealthy, respected, and admired by millions of Americans. Goldwyn understood that the wealth and fame which had come to him as a result of a long and prosperous career in pictures was not an accident. He had worked hard and could take a great deal of self-satisfaction from his many accomplishments.

However, Goldwyn understood that his own life was also an example of the American dream come true. Not just when his career was at an end, but all during it, he took time to thank America for the good life it had given to him and his family. His choice of particularly American institutions, American landscapes, and American themes, not to mention the works of American authors point out vividly his pride in being an American. This is not to say that Goldwyn found America or American society flawless. He reveals these flaws, painfully at some times, in many of his films. Goldwyn was enough of a realist to find fault with his country and enough of a romantic and a patriot to love it regardless.

One of the qualities which Goldwyn admired most about America was the basic goodness of its people and honesty of its institutions. America did not try to hide its failings but rather to expose them

The three veterans returning home: Harold Russell, Dana Andrews and Frederic March in The Best Years of Our Lives.

and correct them. This quality of national self-inspection and the possibility of self-correction infused Goldwyn and his pictures with an overriding sense of optimism.

Many of Goldwyn's feelings about America can be inferred from films discussed in other contexts. In *The Little Foxes,* for example, a money-lust destroys that central American institution, the family. In *Street Scene* and *Dead End,* the social indifference to the existence of slums results in violence and destroyed dreams. In each of these three cases it could be argued that the views expressed are more those of the authors than Goldwyn, the producer. Still, Goldwyn chose to produce these particular works and certainly could have altered any scenes or any views he wished to. His refusal to cover up America's failing coupled with his admiration, indeed love, of America's possibilities led to an ultimate ambivalence best expressed in his masterpiece *The Best Years of Our Lives.* Before he could film his final vision, however, he spent many years refining that vision.

Barbary Coast (1935)

Goldwyn's vision starts with a view of America as a land of exaggerated characteristics; meaner people, truer love, rougher violence, truer retribution. In one sense, *Barbary Coast* is nothing more than a period piece with melodramatic overtones. Yet many themes, however muted, are present. America's fascination with violence, the ability of love to flourish in that violent atmosphere, and the ability of Americans to uproot the source of violence eventually, are all there.

Goldwyn's interest in America had always included a curiosity about the particularly exotic eras of American history which were so foreign to him. He had for several years planned to film a story about the gold rush era in San Francisco. The setting apparently struck him as reflecting the roots of American society and, simultaneously, as providing a background perfect for a producer who relished lavish costumes and realistic sets. Eventually Goldwyn came across a book titled *Barbary Coast* which was set in the proper time and place.

The book itself, written by Herbert Asbury, was not really a story; instead it was a journalistic account of criminal elements of the gold rush era. Goldwyn, who had apparently read neither the book nor a synopsis, simply hired Ben Hecht and Charles MacArthur to take the setting and create a story to fit it. The filming began in May, 1934, but Goldwyn ordered the production stopped several weeks later. In a characteristic fashion, Goldwyn knew he did not like the film but could not say exactly why. He ordered the film to be rewritten and took the two stars originally cast, Gary Cooper and Anna Sten, and put them in *The Wedding Night*. Satisfied that the new script would work Goldwyn began the film again.

The plot line of *Barbary Coast* is one filled with action. A young woman named Mary Rutledge (Miriam Hopkins) arrives in San Francisco from her home in the East to marry her fiance, a gold prospector who has become wealthy. When she arrives in town, Mary learns that her intended was involved in a fight over gambling and is dead. She meets Marcus Aurelius Cobb, who runs San Francisco's first newspaper. Cobb, seeking to protect her, suggests she return to her home in New York. Mary declines. Instead she goes to San Francisco's leading gambling casino, the Bella Donna Club. There she meets Louis Chamalis, the head of the city's underworld (Edward G. Robinson). Enchanted by her, Chamalis asks if she will become the club's hostess. She accepts this offer. Known as Swan, she dresses with diamonds and runs the roulette wheel.

One night at the wheel a Scotch gold prospector named Sandy Ferguson loses his entire stake. When Ferguson claims the wheel is crooked and that he has been cheated out of his money, he is killed. The newspaperman Cobb, anxious to reveal the facts, plans to run a story in his paper about the murder. To prevent this, Chamalis orders Cobb's entire newspaper plant destroyed. Swan interferes, preventing this. Her intervention angers Chamalis who tells her that she will one day be fired.

Swan likes to ride in the fields where gold is searched for. On a ride one day she meets a prospector named Jim Carmichael (Joel McCrea). Carmichael, an idealist, sees how beautiful she is and believes her to be a proper lady. The following evening Carmichael enters the Bella Donna Club. When he sees Swan spinning the roulette wheel his illusions about her are shattered. He begins gambling and, because the game is fixed, loses all his money. Despite the revelation that the beautiful lady is really a gambling hostess, Carmichael understands that he is deeply in love with Swan. She returns the interest and begins to see him on a regular basis. This annoys Chamalis. He orders Carmichael killed.

Before the order can be carried out, however, Chamalis must face a challenge. Sandy Ferguson's partner, Sawbuck McTavish, is killed when he tries to avenge Sandy's murder. Marcus Cobb prints the truth about Chamalis in the newspaper and he, too, is killed.

Following this violence a vigilante committee is formed.

Chamalis then learns that Swan has let Carmichael win back his lost money. When Chamalis's toughest bouncer, Knuckles Jacoby, is hanged by a group of vigilantes, Chamalis decides to kill Carmichael himself. Chamalis goes after Carmichael and Swan on San Francisco Bay. One of Chamalis's men shoots Carmichael. Begging for Carmichael's life, Swan promises that she will go with Chamalis if Carmichael is spared. Chamalis, seeing the two are in love, lets them both go. And as the film ends, Chamalis comes face to face with the vigilantes who have trained their guns at him.

Despite the melodramatic aspects of the film, *Barbary Coast* represented more than a brawling, costume drama. All of the elements that went into the building of America—violence, lust, idealism, fighting corruption—are there though still without coherence. Critical acclaim for the film was not based on these embedded subjects but on the gaudy aspects of the production itself.

The centrality of America as setting was not discussed. Critics did not notice that Swan faced the same potential fate as Nana did in the 1934 movie. Both women engaged in a life of vice. Nana lived in French society and ended a suicide. Swan, however, in an American society marked by the possibility of redemption unavailable in the old-world European setting of Nana, is saved by love. Chamalis, a mean villain throughout the film, changes at the end. The evil of the Bella Donna Club is destroyed by a community vigilante group. This ability of America to right itself is crucial for Goldwyn.

Come and Get It (1936)

Edna Ferber was one popular novelist whom Goldwyn admired because he was convinced that the stories she wrote could survive translation to the screen. He especially liked her novel *Come and Get It*, about lumberjacking in Wisconsin. The novel is very much a description of the American landscape. Goldwyn, however, saw difficulties in transmitting the entirety of that landscape to the screen. He decided to focus on the story, thus taking a step backward from *Barbary Coast*. He seemed not yet ready to handle America directly. He maintained however, a high level of quality for *Come and Get It*, hiring Howard Hawks, well-known for his past successes in adventure films, as director. Edward Arnold, Joel McCrea, and Frances Farmer were hired to be the leads.

Come and Get It was filmed at the same time as *Dodsworth*. During the shooting of the two films Goldwyn underwent prostrate surgery and was unable to oversee day-to-day work or view the daily rushes. *Come and Get It* was looked over by Merritt Hulburd, Goldwyn's associate producer.

As soon as he was released from the hospital, Goldwyn asked to see the two completed films. He ran both films in his home projection room. He was understandably satisfied with *Dodsworth* but very dissatisfied with *Come and Get It*. Without authorization Hawks had ordered that the second half of the film be rewritten. Hawks tried to justify the changes on aesthetic grounds, but Goldwyn had long-established views of a director's prerogatives. "Directors are supposed to direct, not WRITE"[1] Goldwyn informed Hawks. Goldwyn wanted the last half of the film to be redone, but Hawks had an obligation to direct another film (which turned out to be *Bringing Up Baby* with Cary Grant). Goldwyn, after much resistance, turned the task of reshooting over to William Wyler. Wyler depreciated his role and fought with Goldwyn about keeping Hawks's name on the credits as co-director. Goldwyn, however, thought the extra $100,000 he spent to do the reshooting was well worth it; he had a film which was truly his.

Come and Get It takes place in the middle 1880s and centers on the life and struggle of one character, Barney Glasgow. Barney, who oversees a lumber camp, leads a life marked by brawling, wooing barmaids, and trying to become part of the business he works for. With his friend Swan Bostrom, "that crazy Swede," Barney sees a singer named Lotta Morgan in a saloon owned by Sid Le Maire. The singer comes to join him at the roulette wheel and he wins a considerable amount of money. Le Maire tries to force her to get the money back, but Lotta helps the two men escape the saloon by throwing the beer trays at Le Maire's thugs.

Lotta and Barney stay together until Barney's ambition destroys their relationship. Barney decides that his success depends on his marrying his boss's plain daughter, Emma Louise. Barney entrusts his friend Swan to tell Lotta of his decision. Swan makes an impromptu proposal to Lotta and, heartbroken, she accepts.

Barney marries Emma Louise and for many years leads a very unhappy life. His unhappiness is tempered by the fact that he has become a successful lumber tycoon. He has a son who, unlike himself, is honest. His daughter, concerned about only her own pleasure, plans to marry one of her father's workers. He is too indifferent to her and to the rest of his family to care.

Barney's abiding unhappiness finally leads to a decision to see his old friend Swan again. Barney goes back to the original lumber town they both worked in. Swan tells Barney that Lotta has died, but left a daughter, also named Lotta. The daughter, Barney discovers, is as beautiful as her mother once was. When Barney sees her the years disappear and he immediately falls in love with her.

Thinking he might still have an opportunity to have a true love in his life, Barney plots to bring Swan, Lotta, and Lotta's unmarried cousin Karie Linbeck to the city where he now lives. He provides a cottage for them to live in and gives Swan a job which involves pay but no work. Barney then turns his attention to Lotta. After a short while Richard, Barney's son, meets Lotta and he, too, falls in love with her. Father and son become rivals. Barney schemes to get rid of Richard by trying to convince his son to run their new mill in the East. Richard, however, wants to stay and fight for Lotta. Lotta herself thinks of Barney as too old. Finally, Barney realizes that he cannot give up all he has worked for to marry the young girl and he returns to his wife.

The critical reaction to the film was very positive. Howard Barnes, commenting in the *New York Herald Tribune*, wrote: "Essentially it is the brilliant portrayal of the leading role by Edward Arnold that gives the photoplay power and distinction . . . all of the handsome mounting of the film would go for little without [his] splendid realization of Barney."[2] For his supporting role as Swan, a then unknown named Walter Brennan won his first Oscar for Best Actor. There is, of course, a resemblance between *Barbary Coast* and *Come and Get It*. The struggling worker, the girl in the dance hall, and the evil owner are characters in both. But while *Barbary Coast* limits its story line ot these characters, *Come and Get It* expands it considerably. Interestingly, in *Barbary Coast* the lovers are united, while in *Come and Get It* the hero misses out on love twice, essentially with the same woman.

In constructing this melodrama of Barney's life Goldwyn has reduced the background of the original novel in such a way that we do not fully understand the powerful attraction lumber had for a man like Barney. Goldwyn was too concerned with the events in Barney's life to notice the contributing factors that motivated many of those events. Thus *Come and Get It* is easily comparable to earlier and later Goldwyn works about sexual lust, adultery, and cross-generation attraction (as in *Best Years of Our Lives*). Goldwyn still conceived of the American landscape either only as an exotic background or of no crucial relationship to the lives of the characters. He knew, as he demonstrated in the 1931 film *Street Scene*, that cities could have an effect, but he was unable to take himself out of the city or see how heartland America affected American characters.

The Westerner (1940)

The Westerner was Goldwyn's attempt to deal with the myths of an American West a bit more primitive and less dandified than that presented in *Barbary Coast*. In most American films the use of the West in its mythic era—the mid-to-late nineteenth century—resulted in simplistic stories in which the forces of good defeat the forces of evil in a world made uncluttered by the nonexistence of law and civilization. In seeking to avoid that unworthy tradition, Goldwyn attempted to transform the myth: instead of mythical heroes and villains Goldwyn decided to have a story with one realistic character based on a real-life Western judge and one mythic cowboy. This mixture, neither realistic nor completely mythical, does not quite work, but beyond the interesting experiment Goldwyn was clearly moving closer to an appreciaton of the effect that being an American had on a particular character in one of his films.

The historical character is based on Judge Roy Bean, the tyranni-cal, self-appointed "Law West of the Pecos" in the 1880s. Bean was famous for his harsh, often unfair, verdicts and his idolatry of the beautiful British entertainer, Lillie Langtry.

The movie starts out providing the landscape against which the action will take place: a trial which symbolizes the battle between homesteader and cattle breeder. Into this moral chaos—where arbitrary law rules, where order means the intermittent peace between regular range wars—comes the mythic character, "the Westerner," Cole Hardin, played by Gary Cooper.

The Westerner character is entirely within the bounds of the mythic American hero. That hero was a solitary man knowledgeable about evil in the world, capable of understanding it, and, more importantly, capable of defeating it. Part of the way this mythic hero deals with the world, and the evil people in it, is to develop an outer toughness, a seemingly morally indifferent personality combined with an ability to fight. This outer toughness is often incorrectly interpreted by the people this character meets as a lack of ordinary human feeling. On the contrary, however, despite he hero's acknowledgment of the widespread existence of evil in the world, a crucial center of his character is his willingness, bordering on a life's mission, to help out innocent people who are in trouble but incapable of protecting themselves. This, then, is the sort of character that Goldwyn sends into Roy Bean's world of Vingaroon, Texas.

Cole Hardin is arrested for stealing a horse. During the "trial" Hardin discovers that the judge, Roy Bean, is devoted to Lillie Langtry, the famous entertainer, although he has never met her. Hardin casually mentions to Bean, just after Bean had sentenced the Westerner to death, that he knows the English actress quite well. He tells Bean that, although it's not on him, he even owns a lock of Miss Langtry's hair. Staggered by the possibility of obtaining that lock of hair, Bean pardons Hardin.

The two men become friends of sorts. Hardin intervenes with Bean to end the constant fighting between the men who own cattle, who are Bean's supporters, and who need land for their cattle to graze on, and the men who are building homes and farms, who need the same land the cattle need. These homesteaders are led by Caliphet Mathews. Hardin arranges for Bean to declare a truce between the two warring groups.

Hardin falls in love with Jane-Ellen Mathews, Caliphet's daughter and so he joins the landowner's side. This infuriates the judge who decides to revert to his usual method of justice and have Hardin arrested. Bean then recalls the promised lock of hair. Hardin then does deliver the lock—one obtained from Jane-Ellen. Thinking he has averted a war, Hardin is surprised when soon after the cattlemen begin to burn crops and kill Caliphet Mathews. Hardin decides that it is necessary to kill the judge. When he arrives to kill him, Hardin discovers that the judge has gone to see the real Lillie Langtry who is scheduled to appear at Fort Davis. The judge has bought all the tickets for the performance so Lillie will be singing to him alone. Bean seats himself in the first row, hears the overture, and suddenly sees the Westerner before him with a gun. Hardin mortally wounds the judge and then brings him to Miss Langtry so that he might see her before he dies.

The film received mixed reviews. Only the performance of Walter Brennan as Judge Roy Bean was judged superlative. Howard Barnes summed up the view of many critics: "Samuel Goldwyn has lavished his usual high production polish on *The Westerner*, but it hasn't resulted in a particularly entertaining show. Screen horse opera needs action more than atmosphere to be effective . . . . It is probably the fault of the narrative that *The Westerner* is only sporadically entertaining."[3]

The film first fails as historical fact. Judge Roy Bean died a very old man, and not by gunfire, in 1903. He did, in fact, see Lillie Langtry perform in 1888 in San Antonio. No character named Cole Hardin played any part in Bean's notorious life. The film also fails as imaginative fiction. Its mythic elements are too restrained by the very historical realities it distorts. This confusion of the mythic and the historical is mirrored in the film's failure to center on one protagonist; both Brennan and Cooper share that title.

The Westerner is about the taming of America. As such it advances the thesis that such a taming was both inevitable and beneficial. *The Westerner* shows how justice is perverted when its power is arbitrary, when fear and power have displaced established laws. The encroaching civilization—represented in this film by the homesteaders—brings with it order, stability, justice, even love.

In *The Westerner* Goldwyn thought about America as an idea for the first time. His thinking resulted in a confused image of the real America: Was it the land of dreams, freedom, and justice or was it the land of law by the gun and the land where dreams became perverted? Was America represented by Cole Hardin who dreamed of family love and order and honesty or was it represented by Judge Roy Bean who cynically and cruelly ordered men hanged, and dreamed, not of love, but of lust for Lillie Langtry? Goldwyn's inability to settle on a protagonist shows an inability to answer the very question posed by the film. It is as though two very different Americas exist side by side, in uneasy relationship, in the film. Finally, in the film one side is killed off. Despite his inability to create a clear plot which would have resulted from choosing Hardin as the protagonist, Goldwyn does make a tentatively optimistic conclusion about American life, a conclusion that comes too late to save the film.

Pride of the Yankees (1942)

The glimmer of optimism which *The Westerner* ended on becomes fully luminous in *Pride of the Yankees*, a biographical film based on the life of baseball star Lou Gehrig.

In the *Pride of the Yankees*, based on a story written by Paul Gallico, Goldwyn found a story that was fundamentally optimistic about the system of American values. He found such a story by selecting as subject matter the life of the most typical American hero imaginable: a baseball player. Goldwyn knew virtually nothing about the national pastime, which is probably why he refrained

Goldwyn's top star, Gary Cooper, in two legendary roles: (top) with Walter Brennan in William Wyler's The Westerner; *(bottom) as Yankee star Lou Gehrig in* The Pride of the Yankees.

from any fictionalized account. He did know the story of Gehrig, of his physical trials, of how much he was admired, even loved, by the American public.

There were genuine arguments against filming a biography of Gehrig. First, many women in America at the time were not interested in baseball and so would be reluctant to go to a movie with a baseball setting. Second, since baseball was understood well only in America, foreign sales would be drastically curtailed. Third, during production America entered World War II and people had more serious matters on·their mind than sports. Finally, Goldwyn's decision to omit virtually all dramatic baseball scenes to concentrate on Gehrig's life off the field might anger the baseball fans who would make up a large proportion of the audience.

Despite these arguments, Goldwyn saw in Gehrig's life, and perhaps especially in his struggle against disease, a story which typified the best character which America could create. America, Goldwyn would show, could produce a man with physical skill, humor, courage, with a close-knit sense of family who worked hard in a land of opportunity to achieve success.

Goldwyn was convinced from the start that Gary Cooper was the perfect actor for the lead role. This casting led to an unforseen problem. No natural baseball player himself, Cooper could barely bat, throw, or field a baseball as a right-hander. Gehrig, of course, was a left-handed batter and thrower. The dilemma seemed insoluble: either have Cooper looking very obviously awkward in a portrayal of a great player, or change actors, or have Cooper bat and throw right-handed and take the jeers which would inevitably follow. Because of this problem Goldwyn seriously thought of canceling the picture. As was often the case, however, his film was saved by one of the technical experts he had hired. His art director, William Cameron Menzies, suggested a simple solution: print the film backward while Cooper swung and threw right-handed. The trick is nearly impossible to detect, especially because the baseball scenes are quite limited.

The film itself is episodic, using bits and pieces of Gehrig's life to represent his entire life. As a child, he is pictured as already anxious to become a baseball player while his immigrant parents see him as an engineer. Gehrig's mother is employed as a cook by Columbia University. After high school Gehrig enters Columbia. He becomes well-known for his athletic prowess. One day while playing baseball Gehrig is seen by a sportswriter named Sam Blake. Impressed with the young man's talents, Blake goes to the New York Yankees to report on his find. Gehrig, the dutiful son, refuses to join the Yankees when they offer him a job, planning instead the engineering career his parents want. However, when he learns that his mother is in need of an operation which will be very costly, Gehrig decides that the quickest way to get the needed money is to sign with the Yankees. He does so and is sent to the Hartford farm team.

Gehrig continues to deceive his mother into thinking he is studying engineering at Harvard. When he is finally brought up by the Yankees, he is written about in the papers and Mrs. Gehrig discovers the deception. She has a difficult time at first adjusting to the career choice her son had made; she eventually discovers the joys of baseball and becomes an avid fan.

When Gehrig appears for the first time in a game in Chicago he is mocked by a female spectator when he trips over a group of bats. The young woman turns out to be Eleanor Twitchell, the daughter of the Chicago team's owner. Later the two meet at dinner and their romance develops quickly. After the Yankees win the World Series, Gehrig decides that he will propose to Eleanor.

Gehrig's playing for the Yankees is told frequently in newsreel style from long distance shots. He achieves fame for his baseball abilities and is nicknamed "Iron Man" because he never misses a game. One of the numerous incidents in his career involves Gehrig and Babe Ruth visiting a child lying sick in a hospital bed. In front of reporters Ruth promises the boy that he will hit a home run in the boy's honor that day. When the reporters leave, Gehrig promises the boy that he will hit two home runs. Both promises are fulfilled.

Although happily married to Eleanor, Gehrig does have some family problems. His mother continues to try to control his life. She even selects the furniture for the young couple. Eleanor especially resents this interference. When Gehrig confronts his mother about this she says that she respects her son's independence.

During the spring training in 1939 Gehrig notices difficulty in swinging his bat and his performance suffers. He notices the progressive difficulties and finally asks to be taken out of the line-up, ending his record of appearing in 2,130 consecutive games. When he goes to see doctors concerning his condition he is told that he has a neurological disease. The doctors tell him that he has only a few years to live. He leaves the Yankees and tries to prevent Eleanor from discovering how fatal the disease (amytropic multiple sclerosis) is. She, however, learns the truth.

On July 4, 1939, with Eleanor's help, the Yankees have a "Lou Gehrig Appreciation Day." With newsreel footage and process shots we see Gehrig on the verge of tears telling the crowd: "Some people say I've had a bad break, but today I consider myself the luckiest man on the face of the earth."

There was considerable critical acclaim for the picture. *Variety* for example, claimed that "Samuel Goldwyn has produced a stirring epitaph . . . [and] Gary Cooper blends neatly into a hero's role. Gehrig is depicted for what he was, a quiet, plodding personality who strived for and achieved perfection in his profession." *Time* called it "A typical U.S. success story."[4] The film received ten Academy Award nominations (eventually winning only one, for best editing).

One of the major weaknesses in the film is that there is little dramatic conflict. For a while Gehrig's mother cannot accept his occupation; for an even shorter while his wife-to-be makes fun of him. But these conflicts are both minor and short-lived. Gehrig encounters no important conflict in the entire movie. It is precisely a conflict, though, that should have been the dramatic center: Gehrig's conflict about death. He is shown to exemplify a simple heroism. There is no real fear, no anger about his illness. None of the emotions humans feel are in the film. *Pride of the Yankees* becomes almost a paean to stoicism in the face of death, and, by implication, to the particularly American ethos that makes such a stoicism possible. Some self-doubt on Gehrig's part, or even on Eleanor's part, would have added to the virtually nonexistent dramatic qualities of the movie.

Although the picture was seen, and reviewed, as a tribute to Gehrig and to America, the optimism about the American Way of Life does have some limitations. Interestingly, Goldwyn chose to film Gehrig's life rather than, say, Babe Ruth's, a man who was even more of a legend, and who was still alive at the time of the filming (who, indeed, appeared as an actor in the film). Goldwyn's choice of Gehrig rather than Ruth or any of hundreds of other possible symbols of the kind of person America could develop is illuminating. In Goldwyn's vision of the American myth the hero still dies. The myth is never allowed to transcend the real world. This is no fully idealized America.

Goldwyn is more aware of the effect of being an American in *Pride of the Yankees* than he had been in previous films. His ambivalent attitude toward America, though, still had not found a means of expression. Just as it took him many films to draw out his complete vision of love and marriage, so, too, he had to go from film to film experimenting with the permutations resulting from a mixture of the American myth and American reality. He still had not found the perfect combination after finishing *Pride of the Yankees.*

The Best Years of Our Lives (1946)

It was with the making of *The Best Years of Our Lives* that Samuel Goldwyn reached his pinnacle as a producer. The film both sums up and symbolizes his career. Additionally, Goldwyn finally crystallizes his views about America in the film.

The story of the making of *The Best Years of Our Lives* starts with an August, 1944, issue of *Time* magazine which featured a discussion of one of the many problems brought on by the war—the difficult readjustments veterans faced when they returned home from battle.

The Goldwyns were sitting in their living room. Frances Goldwyn was reading the *Time* issue. What she found especially interesting, in addition to the human interest of the story, was an accompanying photograph. The picture showed a group of marines leaning out a window of a railway car. The car had a sign painted on it: "Home Again!" The gist of the story was that the men were unhappy because of the problems that awaited them in civilian life: dealing with physical handicaps, with the dull routine of their prewar lives, and the possible tension with families, wives, and girl friends from whom they had been separated.

Frances showed the article to her husband, and Goldwyn agreed that it made an excellent basis for a movie story. He realized that the key to making a good film from the article would be in finding a qualified writer. His favorites were unavailable; he and Lillian Hellman were no longer on speaking terms, and Sidney Howard had died. Most other qualified writers were serving in the armed forces.

Goldwyn finally hit upon MacKinlay Kantor, whose historical books about the Civil War period had been turned into films. (Kantor's masterpiece, *Andersonville*, had not yet been written.) Kantor's agent had contacted Goldwyn about script work, but until the idea of the problems of returning veterans came along, Goldwyn had not been able to use Kantor. In this case, Goldwyn decided that a writer learned in history and military life, and who had spent some time in England as an air force correspondent, would be a perfect choice.

Goldwyn called Kantor on the same night on which he had read the story. The two reached a verbal agreement: Kantor would write a screen treatment for $10,000. It took Kantor six months, until January, 1945, to complete the project. Instead of a screen treatment, however, Kantor wrote a novel in blank verse about three returning soldiers. Goldwyn considered the novel, *Glory for Me*, impossible to film. He decided to accept the loss of his investment and forget the film.

During the brief remainder of the war Goldwyn concentrated on other film projects. After the war many of Hollywood's writers and directors returned. One of the returning directors was William Wyler, who had been making films for the army air force. Wyler owed Goldwyn one more picture according to a contract. Goldwyn offered him some films but Wyler turned them down.

Wyler, once a wild, carefree man, had been affected deeply by the war. "The war," he wrote, "had been an escape into reality. In the war it didn't matter how much money you earned. The only thing that mattered were human relationships; not money, not position, not even family. Only relationships with people who might be dead tomorrow were important."[5] Wyler had lost the hearing in his left ear, a loss providing a perspective on soldiers with serious disabilities. Because of his experience, Wyler no longer wished to make the sort of films he had made prior to the war, but rather to use those experiences. He asked Goldwyn to allow him a chance to direct a film about the war. Goldwyn then told Wyler about *Glory for Me*, including his interest in the material but his dissatisfaction with the Kantor novel.

Wyler liked the story told in the novel and wanted to film it. Goldwyn, having given up on the project, tried to divert Wyler's attention by getting him interested in a biographical film written by Robert Sherwood. Wyler and Sherwood discussed the biographical piece and, in the course of the discussion, Wyler mentioned *Glory for Me* to Sherwood.

Sherwood became interested, so he and Wyler went back to Goldwyn, who, seeing how much they liked it, and sensing a confirmation of the appeal he had always found in the material, reconsidered. He assigned Sherwood the job of writing.

Goldwyn's initial advice was simply not to be too "radical." Goldwyn, of course, was aware that inherent in the idea was a display of some flaws in the system of integrating the veteran into society, but he said bluntly: "Just don't knock America." That is to say, Goldwyn was willing to display flaws so long as it was clear that the country itself could correct those flaws, that the country itself was good, albeit with some moral lapses which it could and would attend to. In keeping with his own warning Goldwyn dismissed several of Sherwood's ideas, including a housing riot, saying "I don't want you to think of this as a Hollywood picture. I want something simple and believable."[6]

Richard Griffith notes that Sherwood believed that such advice permitted the ordinary, everyday qualities that emerged in *Best Years* to take precedence over the possible melodrama which would have resulted from filming some of Sherwood's ideas.[7]

After a number of such discussions, Sherwood set about to rework Kantor's verse novel. Wyler especially felt that the spastic character from Kantor's work might appear inadvertently humorous. After considering what other disability might be used, Wyler and Sherwood suggested an amputee. They had seen a short film used by the army which starred a sergeant who had lost his hands. The sergeant in that army film, Harold Russell, demonstrated how agile he was at using hooks. (Russell had been injured at a training mishap in North Carolina involving a premature dynamite explosion.) Wyler and Sherwood then visited a veterans hospital. They came away convinced that, if at all possible, the film role should be portrayed by a real amputee, rather than an actor.

Goldwyn considered all these suggestions, including one that Harold Russell, who seemed quite natural in front of a camera and who could demonstrate to audiences how capable an amputee could be, might be a suitable actor in the film; finally he accepted both the idea of using an amputee and of hiring Russell for the part.

Even though the casting of Harold Russell was accomplished with a minimum of bickering, that did not prevent Goldwyn and Wyler from having their usual fierce arguments about the rest of the cast. They had agreed on Myrna Loy to play Milly Stephenson, the wife of the returning banker, but the original role was small. Goldwyn told Sherwood to add to Milly's character so that Goldwyn could interest the actress in the part. Finally, Dana Andrews and Frederic March were selected for the two other male leads.

Goldwyn found the character of Fred Derry—the Dana Andrews part—to be the most interesting. In both the Kantor and Sherwood versions, Derry returns home from fighting and discovers his wife committing adultery. He ends their relationship. Later in the story, when he meets Peggy Stephenson, he is free to pursue and marry her. This lack of drama bothered Goldwyn. It was not a lack in action so much as in dramatic tension. He did not see why he was bothered at the time, although from a distance it seems more obvious: his notion of drama involving adultery invariably involved a moral man torn between a nagging wife and a more vital, more alive woman. The tension between moral qualms and passion was at the center of an adultery drama in the Goldwyn tradition. Thus it is no surprise that Goldwyn finally found one of Sherwood's suggestions acceptable: Derry would not discover his wife's adultery right away.

With this change Goldwyn had altered his notion of a love triangle. In *Best Years* the drama—the love triangle—is based on the fact that Fred can not fall in love with Peggy as long as he is married, and yet early on we sense that he finds his wife to be a stranger. That is his moral dilemma.

Finally, an acceptable script was completed. By the time of the script's completion, however, Goldwyn began to worry again. He was not worried about the two million dollars he planned to spend on the movie, but about the delay in having made the film. Hollywood insiders insisted that Goldwyn was too late in making a war-related film, that, in the aftermath of the war, audiences were interested in light entertainment. The character portrayed by Harold Russell was looked on particularly as a major blunder on Goldwyn's part because, it was thought, audiences would be repulsed.

Realizing just how extraordinary his film would be, but curious about the accuracy of the gossip, Goldwyn decided to contact the Audience Research Institute to discover if, indeed, moviegoers were adverse to the subject matter he was planning to present or if they had had enough of films about returning veterans.

Such an action on Goldwyn's part was almost unheard of in Hollywood at the time, and it serves to underscore his willingness not only to be a rebel, to gamble on his audience's intelligence, but also to push forward his mature views. He was creating a work, he knew, that solved the emotional and intellectual problems he had devoted his artistic life to solving, and he was not about to shelve that film because Hollywood gossips told him to. He needed reassurance, perhaps, but it is possible that he would have gone ahead and made the film whatever the results of the Institute's findings. At any rate, the survey demonstrated that audiences were still concerned about the problems of returning veterans.

Filming for *The Best Years of Our Lives* took just under four months. Four hundred thousand feet of film were shot from the one hundred and ninety page script.

Wyler, following Goldwyn's dictum to make this a picture about ordinary life, a picture packed with human drama, came to several crucial decisions in conferences with Goldwyn. The film would be shot in black and white instead of the color stock popular in other films of the time. This decision was based on a belief that black and white would present a grimmer, tougher world, a more realistic representation of the world the characters in the movie inhabited. Color, it was decided, was meant for happier, more upbeat movies, or for purely entertainment films. In addition, the film's costume designer, Irene Sharaff, was told to dispense with the usual practice of designing and making costumes. Instead the "costumes" were ordinary clothes bought in a department store. The actors wore the store-bought clothes for several weeks prior to filming. Finally, as he had in previous important films, Goldwyn made the entire cast rehearse as though they were preparing a play.

After the film was completed, it was cut to sixteen thousand feet, more than twice as long as a film's usual length. At first Goldwyn wanted to cut the film in half in order to make distribution easier (so that the extra costs of distributing a long film would not have to be made up by charging a high admission price). However, after viewing the film in its entirety, Goldwyn realized the stories told in the film needed time and space to complete their telling. Goldwyn realized there was no excess footage; the tough-minded producer could not find any artistic justification for reducing the film's length. Unsure that two hours and forty minutes was an acceptable length for a film with so realistic a subject matter, Goldwyn decided to hold a sneak preview of the film in October, 1946. The preview audience reacted as he had; they loved the film.

Several titles for the film appealed to him, and so, once again, he decided to test his taste against an audience's. When the audience chose from the various titles offered them *The Best Years of Our Lives*, Goldwyn seemed delighted. Goldwyn found that his taste was still very similar to the taste of the average viewer both in terms of subject matter and titling.

The film opened at the Astor Theater in New York on November 22, 1946. At first Goldwyn planned on a January West Coast premiere, only at the last moment deciding to open in Los Angeles in December so as to qualify for the 1946 Academy Awards.

The story in *The Best Years of Our Lives* centers about three returning veterans who meet while waiting to take a plane home to the city in which they live. The three end up traveling together to Boone City, and, once there, taking a taxi to their respective residences. The three veterans are Al Stephenson, who is returning to his upper-class life as a banker after spending the war years as an infantry sergeant commanding men from socially lower classes; Fred Derry, an air force pilot and war hero who is returning to his bride, but, he hopes, not to his old civilian job as a soda-jerk; and Homer Parrish, who, while serving in the Navy, has lost both of his hands, which have been replaced by hooks.

Homer is the first to be dropped off on the ride. He is disturbed by the possible reactions of his family, but especially of his girl friend from before the war, Wilma Caroron. Homer's mother cries as she sees the hooks, but his family and Wilma, who lives next door to the Parrishes, provide an enthusiastic welcome for him. He feels uncertain about them and suspects that their kindness originates from pity.

Al is next to be dropped off. Al's shy, understanding wife Milly, his grown-up, pretty daughter Peggy, and his son Rob await him. He is surprised by his children's growth. Because they have become more adult, he feels unsure around them. Al has learned to celebrate all occasions, and to escape by drinking, and he reacts to the anxiety he feels on his return by having a drink.

Fred Derry leaves the cab last. He goes to his old house and discovers that his wife is not there.

The three returning veterans next meet again in Butch's Bar. Al, Milly, and Peggy Stephenson have gone there to continue celebrating Al's return. Homer is the owner's nephew and stops at the bar regularly. Fred ends up stopping in the bar for a drink, too. He still has not been able to locate his wife.

Fred and Al get drunk at the bar. Fred immediately notices how pretty young Peggy is. Because Fred is so drunk and has no home to go to, the Stephensons decide to take Fred back to their house to let him sleep off his drunk. While there he has a nightmare about a plane's wing catching fire. In the dream the plane is going out of control. Peggy, hearing Fred call out, comforts him, and he feels better.

The next day Fred's drunken father tells him that Marie, Fred's

wife, was forced to leave the house and take an apartment down-
town because of a lack of money. Marie, a pretty blonde Fred
married only a few days prior to his going into service, has taken a
job as a singer in a nightclub. Marie, embittered by her poverty,
stresses to Fred, when they meet again, that she wants him to get a
good job which pays a lot of money. Fred is very much aware of the
disparity between his low-paying work in the drug store, and the
status he achieved in the air force. His uniform becomes a symbol of
that status. Marie does not want him to wear regular clothes. Fred
begins to sense that perhaps Marie is losing interest in a husband
without glamour, without a high-paying job, and without hopes for
improvement in the future.

After finding his wife, Fred sets out to get a job. He goes back to
the drug store to get his prewar position back but finds that his job
has been given to a younger man. Fred is offered $32.50 a week to
be assistant floor manager and to spend part of his time behind the
soda fountain.

Al is appointed vice-president at the bank. He is put in charge of
making loans to veterans.

Homer feels he is no longer the sort of man Wilma should marry.
Even when she tells him that she loves him, he thinks she is lying,
that she feels guilty and is showing him tenderness and pity, not
love. He cannot believe she could love a man without hands. When
she tells him that she still wants to marry him, he is unsure of his
feelings. When he suddenly sees his little sister Luella spying on
Wilma and him through a window, his frustration boils over and he
uses his mechanical "hands" to break a window.

Fred has found solace away from his wife by seeing Peggy. He
finds in her a woman concerned about his health and his readjustment, a woman who cares about him as a person, not about his
image, or the type of job he has. The two go out tentatively, but
eventually begin an affair. Peggy tells him that Marie wanted a
"smooth operator," a man agile in gaining success whether or not
that success was morally achieved. Peggy tells him that he is not
that sort of man, and that Marie ought not to have such expectations
of him.

Homer visits Fred in the drugstore and gets into a fight about the
war. Fred throws a punch and is fired.

Al, meanwhile, is having a difficult time on his job. Because he
has dealt with poor people in the service, he has come to recognize
when they are being honest. He recommends a loan be given to a

Goldwyn's masterpiece: Theresa Wright, Myrna Loy, and Dana Andrews in The Best Years of Our Lives.

veteran who can offer no collateral. Al's superiors at the bank are surprised by his approval, and he tries to tell them that men like the one he gave the loan to needed work and could not get it without taking a loan. He suggests that honesty is a better collateral than property. Later, at a dinner in his honor, he continues this theme in a drunken speech attacking the bank and advocating more social responsibility.

Homer has made a decision about Wilma. He plans to show her how he puts on and takes off his hooks. He tells her that he loves her but then he says: "You don't know Wilma what it would be like to live with me, to have to face this [he lifts his hooks] every day, every night." She responds: "I can only find out by trying, and if it turns out I haven't got courage enough, well, we'll soon know." Homer takes Wilma to his bedroom and removes the hooks. Wilma calmly looks on. When the demonstration is finished, Wilma has convinced Homer of her true feelings, and the couple plan to wed.

In contrast, Fred's marriage is about to fall apart. He returns home and finds his wife with a boy friend, an ex-marine. She announces that she is leaving. She says she has given him the best years of her life, but that he is a failure.

While waiting to find another job, Fred visits a site where airplanes that are no longer useful are lined up waiting to be scrapped. Fred, who has earned a Distinguished Flying Cross, climbs into the cockpit of a B-17. He sits there thinking of his days as a bombardier. He seems to realize that like the plane he has outlived his usefulness. A workman then orders Fred to get out of the plane, but, after talking, offers Fred a job.

The final scene of the film is set at Homer and Wilma's marriage. As Homer places the wedding ring on Wilma's finger, Fred asks Peggy to marry him, and she agrees.

The reviews were unanimous. Bosley Crowther, the *New York Times* critic, summed up the critical acclaim: "It is seldom that there comes a motion picture which can be wholly and enthusiastically endorsed not only as superlative entertainment but as food for quiet and humanizing thought. Having to do with a subject of large moment . . . and cut, as it were, from the heartwood of contemporary American life, this film . . . does a great deal more, even, than the above. It gives off a warm glow of affection for every-day, down-to-earth folks."[8]

Photographer Gregg Toland was particularly praised, and not only by critics. William Wyler said of him: "Gregg Toland's remarkable facility for handling background and foreground action has enabled me . . . to develop a better technique of staging my scenes . . . I can have action and reaction in the same shot without having to cut back and forth from individual cuts of the characters. This makes for smooth continuity, an almost effortless flow of scene, for much more interesting composition in each shot, and lets the spectator look from one to the other character at his own will, do his own cutting."[9]

An example of the kind of scene Wyler is talking about here takes places in Butch's Bar. Fred Derry is in the background talking in a phone booth. He is calling Peggy to end their relationship. In the foreground Al is leaning over while Butch and Homer are playing the piano.

Although praise for Toland was unanimous, some critics thought Wyler's explanation disingenuous. Andre Bazin, for instance, liked the photographic principle thinking it more "democratic" than shallow focus—in which only the background or foreground, but not both, is in focus—for the same reason as Wyler: a number of important characters could be shown simultaneously and the viewer could choose which character to observe. Bazin, however, says of both *Best Years* and *The Little Foxes*—in which the technique had also been used,—that "Wyler had effectively determined which characters the spectators would be interested in, by the moral and emotional traits with which he endowed them, and which he balances one against the other. . . ." Bazin, of course, identified the development of the story's characters with the director when, in this case, the producer was crucial in deciding the traits Bazin considers important. Bazin's notion, however, of a democratic deep-focus is particularly appealing insofar as it applies to *The Best Years of Our Lives*. Such a photographic technique supports the essential message of the film and may explain the seemingly perfect marriage of form and content in the film. Of course, even with several characters and numerous objects for a viewer to choose from, the camera, like any other artistic device, still choses a range for the audience to see.

Even in a nonvisual artistic medium, such as music or, especially, literature, the artist selects the characters present on a scene, gives them an appearance, dialogue, and setting, and selects a tone to lead readers to form emotional attitudes toward the characters. The nature of the artistic enterprise, however, is not merely to represent the world as a world would be represented by an image in a mirror, but, instead, to make some statement about the natural or social world, or to create an imaginative world; and this requires guiding an audience, leading so that the audience can finally share certain visions. In such guiding it is perhaps inevitable that the particular arranging of scenes by the artist is intentional in order to convey a feeling or attitude.

A totally "democratic" camera results not in the democratization of film, but in the loss of artistic control. The real artistic question, then, is not whether or not there should be this guiding, but rather just how much guiding there should be and how obtrusive the artist as guide should be.

With shots of single characters, the guiding is more obvious, more obtrusive. With a shot populated by several characters, and filmed with numerous objects, it is harder for the artist to guide the viewer because there is so much information available it is hard for the artist to be sure that the particular information intended for conveyance is received. A complex art involves this populated shot, with each object, each character, conveying in complementary form the overall information the artist intends to provide.

Not all critics viewed *Best Years* as a masterpiece. James Agee struggled over the film for several weeks in his *Nation* column. He started out by recounting the film's virtues.

Agee admired first of all the quality of writing in the screenplay. He noted the dialogue's smoothness—often the sign of a movie meant to be purely entertaining—was secondary to the action of the film itself, action more meaningful than the dialogue. Agee also praised two long-time Goldwyn collaborators, William Wyler and Gregg Toland. He admired Wyler's war-learned sense of control, and ranks Toland's photography among the best.

Agee, however, makes a distinction between form and content. While he is satisfied that, in its form, *The Best Years of Our Lives* is as good as a film can.be in certain aspects, he is unsettled by its content. He regards much of the film as false. Most striking to Agee is the plotting involving Fred's wife Marie. People in *Best Years*, Agee argues, act in ways too limited for the personalities they have. If they existed in real life their range of behavior would be much wider. If Agee is correct here, then Goldwyn has failed even in his masterpiece to overcome a problem that had long plagued him: an overemphasis on story line at the expense of character development. In other films the solutions were too coincidental, too simple, the human reactions too pat, too obviously serving the story line. If Marie is seen by Agee as too cardboard a character, too obviously set up for the convenience of the story, it is possible to argue that in Marie, and in *Best Years* in general, Goldwyn has finally overcome the problem of character simplicity. To say this it is necessary to argue that a character like Marie could have existed, and that in real life her reactions would have borne a clear resemblance to the character in the film. Richard Griffith most forcefully takes his approach, arguing that Marie could be real, and, by implication, that Agee's main argument against the film fails. Griffith claims: "Marie is just the sort of girl Derry would have married. . . . She is not, as alleged, a character from a Hollywood script-file, but a girl whose values have been shaped by Hollywood."[10]

Like Agee, Robert Warshow believes the movie has a surface reality but underneath is full of untruths, especially in its unclear understanding of the inequalities of political life, and the insufficiency of a personal moral response to social problems. Warshow seems to yearn for a less literary (story-oriented) more documentary (message-oriented) film, or at least of imparting a message winnowed of the era's clichés. The lack of precision in the social message in *Best Years* simply emphasizes that Goldwyn's great strength lay in his telling the stories of ordinary people without intending to impart a social message, but having that message inevitably conveyed by the very circumstances of the characters' lives. To deny reality to the characters, then, as Agee does, is really a much more potentially devastating blow than that attempted by Warshow.

Goldwyn's genius, as suggested by Griffith in his analysis of Marie, is that Goldwyn created ordinary not literary characters. Ordinary characters, common people, are sometimes easily typed by the commonness of the image they present to the world and the "philosophy of life" they choose to live by. Marie is a character like this. Her character is not as complex as Fred's, perhaps, precisely because he has gone off the war and she hasn't. Goldwyn's theory of entertainment included these ordinary people in trying situations to see their reactions.

Agee's real argument is not with Marie, not with Goldwyn, but with the very legitimacy of popular culture, in which the ordinary person in extraordinary circumstances becomes the subject matter. Goldwyn had made his choice in favor of popular culture, and in *Best Years* he provides his best portrait of ordinary Americans at a crucial point in their lives, and in the life of their culture. For Goldwyn such a picture, combined with high quality, was the very definition of filmmaking.

Another argument against the supposed realism of *Best Years* was that its solutions were limited to the immediate problems raised by the film, i.e. that it is a period piece.

Against such a charge, Richard Griffith argues that if *Best Years* offered the social solutions necessary to make it appear more realistic, it would only then have become immediately dated, consigned to film histories as a very good film about the problems returning veterans had after World War II. Instead, the film resonates with a more timeless sound of human adjustment, of the trials of love, of pursuing justice. These are problems faced by all people at all times. Too much realism would have reduced the scope of the film by making an aesthetic product into a social document.[11]

Despite the concerns of some critics *Best Years* was a huge success. The film made eleven million dollars in its first few years. Of more significance to Goldwyn, though, was the fact that *Best Years* won an Academy Award for Best Picture of the Year. The film received seven Academy Awards altogether (it had received eight

nominations). Wyler won for Best Director, Frederic March for Best
Actor, and Harold Russell for Best Supporting Actor. That night at
the Academy Awards Goldwyn also received the Irving Thalberg
Award "for that producer whose creativity over the years reflects
consistently high quality of motion picture production."

The quality of *Best Years* had been officially recognized, but the
quality of the film was only part of its appeal. The film was also
recognized for the effect it would have on the future of motion
pictures and on the general public. The *Los Angeles Times*, for
example, carried an editorial which read: "*The Best Years of Our
Lives* represents the better American spirit. It deserves to be seen
by people throughout today's chaotic world. It typifies the kind of
life most people know and understand in this country. It is not
linked with the gangsters and racketeering so often exploited in the
homegrown cinemas, and which give such a false idea of
America."[12]

This editorial hints at Goldwyn's vision of America, and how that
vision should be presented by motion pictures. Goldwyn's vision
neither glossed over the inequities or difficulties in American life
(which he presented graphically in such films as *Dead End*) nor
dismissed the simple, humane virtues nourished by the American
ethic (which he presented in such films as *Pride of the Yankees*). He
tried for a balance, exaggerating neither the faults nor virtues of his
country. In avoiding the exaggeration of the most sensational
characteristic of American life—violence—because films about violence exaggerated American weaknesses, instead of presenting the
weaknesses in their real dimensions, Goldwyn stayed away from the
gangster films almost entirely. Goldwyn wanted his films to present
social conditions that needed changing, but he did not sensationalize
those conditions so that he might sell more tickets. This balance is
perfectly achieved in *The Best Years of Our Lives:* the themes
Goldwyn explored in *Best Years* were familiar to him and to his
audiences.

One theme he dealt with was the terrible feelings which emerge
when one feels trapped. Goldwyn felt sorry for the person who felt
trapped, whether by a marriage, an environment, social mores, the
law, or something else. Throughout his life and film career, Goldwyn
felt a sympathy for the person who would not or could not escape
the physical or psychological limits which inhibited freedom. In
films such as *Dead End* and *Street Scene* such concerns are most
obvious, but the concern is there in all the films.

In *The Best Years of Our Lives* the characters are trapped in a variety of ways. Fred Derry is trapped by the glory of his own recent past. He is unable to adjust for a long while to his dull present, in which he is not regarded as a hero and in which he finds himself in a job he detests and in a marriage to a woman he barely knows and who is dissatisfied with him.

Maria Derry is trapped by her lust for the material trappings of glamour and success. She hungers for money, not for its own sake, but for how she will then appear to others. (That is why she wants Fred to keep wearing his uniform, telling him that when he does he looks more like himself.)

Homer Parrish is trapped by his anxiety over the loss of his hands and the effect that loss will have on his relationship with the woman he loves. He believes that his loss renders him unmanly and an object of simultaneous horror and pity to Wilma and to his family.

Al Stephenson is trapped at one level by drink, but, underneath that, he is trapped by the conflict he feels between his social conscience and the unconscionable requirements of his job. He is supposed to behave in a detached, objective manner regarding the giving out of loans. Because of his service experiences he wants to provide money for all honest and hard-working applicants.

The variety of entrapments in *Best Years* is important because, after having made a number of films about each different trap, Goldwyn finally could compress all the traps into one film, and, by the end of the film, discuss how all these traps are either escaped from or how they remain permanently ensnaring.

In *Best Years* each of the characters has overcome the limitations placed upon him or her. In all cases (except, perhaps, for Marie) a liberation from the trap leads to at least a tentative happiness which Goldwyn intimates will be permanent. Godwyn's essential message, then, is finally one of optimism, that limitations can be overcome. Fred will marry Peggy; Homer and Wilma do get married; Al's repressed social conscience is loosed in a fury of words.

Sometimes, though, total liberation from a given circumstance is impossible. Under such conditions the ability to adjust is crucial. This idea—so prominent in *Street Scene*—is developed in *Best Years* too, most especially through the character of Homer. Homer's handicap could have resulted in a long-term depression or even a suicide. Instead, Homer, after a difficult period of adjustment, accepts his fate and learns not only how to live with it, but how to teach others to live with it as well. The dramatic scene in which

Homer shows Wilma how his hooks work is, instead of grotesque, a scene of great tenderness.

Another important Goldwyn theme is that the search for love is very difficult. In *Best Years* Goldwyn explores and sums up all the variations on that theme that he had worked on in previous films.

In *Best Years* there are example of love facing severe tests. The two best examples of that test being passed are Milly Stephenson, who stands by her husband despite his drinking and his tortured conscience, and Wilma, who is unwavering in her devotion to Homer, a devotion based on love rather than sympathy. Wilma is perhaps the only flat character in the movie; her love is not truly tested because she never doubts it. In contrast to Milly and Wilma, Marie is an adulteress who cannot accept a life that is ordinary. By the end of the film Marie seems to find her own kind of happiness.

Interestingly, it is the women in the film who seem to define the success or failure of the men's search for love, not particularly the men themselves. The men want love and need it to survive, but, instead of working for it, they expect it. Al and Homer, in fact, make up the test love must face by being the kinds of men they are. Fred and Marie each make up part of their test.

More than in previous pictures, then, *Best Years* places a considerable amount of blame for difficulties in love relationships on the man. By contrast, in *Dodsworth* the test was entirely made by Fran. The asymmetry of this view in the Derry relationship allows Goldwyn to maintain a sense of complexity, to assign blame where appropriate. Nevertheless, in *Best Years* Goldwyn seems to stress the culpability of the male.

The importance of searching for justice, another important Goldwyn theme, is, finally, a matter subordinated to an individual's search for love. Before *Best Years* Goldwyn only rarely saw the connection in his films between the trapped individual and the social system, between the need for love and an alienating society. He recognized that social systems could be inequitable or even dangerous (he was, for example, aware of the dangers of German Fascism from its beginnings), but he was not, as an artist, interested in social institutions as much as he was interested in the lives of ordinary people. It was only when those institutions directly and obviously affected ordinary people that Goldwyn became interested in them. An example of such a direct effect was the effect the service had on returning veterans. Goldwyn was willing to point out the weaknesses in those American institutions which did not help the returning veteran adequately, precisely because Goldwyn was convinced that those democratic institutions were self-correcting, that by pointing out the problems he would, in effect, be solving them.

One of these crucial social problems Goldwyn discussed in *Best Years* that was very controversial was the inadequate incomes the veterans received and how such incomes affected average people. The problem of economic security for the returning veterans had been a subject in previous pictures but Arthur Knight finds no film "more searching or honest" on this subject than *Best Years*.[13]

Marie Derry lives for money and what it can buy. Part of Fred's inability to adjust to civilian life is the result of his low-paying job at the drug store. The turnabout in Fred's life only begins when he gets another job. Al Stephenson, ironically the character with the fewest financial problems, is the character who most clearly and forcefully speaks up about the financial insecurities of the veterans.

Unfortunately, .*Best Years* presents a very one-sided view; the struggle that emerges in Al is between a trusting humanism and a cruel, unyielding economic institution. In oversimplifying the complexity of economic institutions and in sentimentalizing the American situation, Goldwyn duplicated weaknesses found in his previous films. Still, the sentimentality of previous films is mostly under control in this film, especially in its telling of Homer's story.

Goldwyn never defined what he wanted in a good society beyond the politically liberal clichés of his era: he wanted a society in which each individual was free to explore, to create, to get a desired and worthwhile job, the express love openly with whomever one wished to, a society which did not suffocate the optimistic elements in human nature—hope, humor, and expectation. America, when it was at its best, was a living definition of such a society.

The Best Years of Our Lives is a film which, despite some uncertainty about why so great a country should have the serious problems it has, is, at its most profound level, a hymn to the greatness of America. Only on the surface, to an unsophisticated critical eye, could the problem raised by the film be interpreted as anti-American.

8

The Goldwyn Legacy

A Summation

THE BEST YEARS OF OUR LIVES, though not Goldwyn's final film, was the high point of his film career. Although he made a dozen additional pictures, his artistic vision was never again so clear, his subject matter never again so vital.

It was after making *Hans Christian Andersen* in 1952, his seventy-eighth independent production, that Goldwyn decided to reduce his output. For almost forty years he had released between one and three films a year. He waited three years before releasing his next film, *Guys and Dolls*, and until 1959 to release his final film, *Porgy and Bess*.

After *Porgy and Bess*, Goldwyn entered complete retirement. For a decade he lived quietly until he suffered a paralyzing stroke in 1969. From then until his death five years later he had limited use of speech and was confined to a wheelchair.

In March, 1971, President Richard Nixon awarded Goldwyn the Medal of Freedom, the highest award that can be received by a civilian. That, on top of the Thalberg Award and the Jean Hershholt Humanitarian Award he had won in 1957, certified the public recognition of how much a motion picture producer can contribute to a society.

After being released from a Santa Monica, California, hospital in January, 1974, Goldwyn returned home, where on January 31, at two o'clock in the morning, he died.

His death—after those of the other early movie moguls—ended an era in Hollywood, an era in which one strong-willed producer could make quality pictures over the course of a career. Indeed, *Variety* wrote in its obituary that Goldwyn was the "Dean of independent producers, and the only true indie, [who] began

A Goldwyn Gift to Comedy: Eddie Cantor in Whoopee! *(1930)*   167
(Courtesy: Museum of Modern Art/Film Stills Archive)

bucking the majors at a time when they dominated the industry. That he succeeded in the rough competition that existed to an even greater degree in the predivorcement days (before film companies were forced by the courts, in 1948, to divest themselves of their distribution arms) and emerged as a dominant personality among giants commanding vast producing theater-owning combines, he attributed to one factor: having met his competition with a long string of superior quality pictures.''[1]

Beyond the pictures themselves, the Goldwyn legacy is made up of a challenge to filmmakers to make quality pictures despite a temptation to pander to public taste in the least expensive fashion, to use literature as a proper model for film while maintaining each one's autonomy, and to maintain a social conscience by remembering how devastating life and its problems can be to the human personality.

Goldwyn was no theorist and no writer. He left neither confessions nor guidebook. The only guidance we have to Goldwyn's ideas, finally, emerges from a viewing of the films. It was rare in a Goldwyn film to have a truly memorable plot. But the ordinary characters, their plights, their hopes, their reactions to love, and stress, and danger, are endlessly fascinating.

To tell the stories of these characters, Goldwyn took great care in all the aspects of his productions, aspects he himself took charge of. To find characters with interesting stories, Goldwyn turned to literature—novels, stories, and plays. It was in the literary world that he found the people he wished to film, believing the literary artist to be the best observer and truest recorder of the depths of the human soul.

In his passion to create, Goldwyn redefined the notion of producer, a redefinition that, perhaps, has yet to be fully acknowledged. Unlike other producers of his time, Goldwyn saw himself not merely as one contributor to the overall aesthetic product or as a polite suggester of occasional ideas to the film's director. Goldwyn was central to the inception, development, and conclusion of all his films. He made the producer not only one of many contributors to a film, but the key one, the definer of what the film would be. Goldwyn's notion of the producer as the genuine creator, the genuine "author," of the film, allows for an expanded interpretation of what has come to be known as the auteur theory.

Adherents of this aesthetic theory believe that a director is to a film as an author is to a book, and that all aesthetic qualities ascribed to a film, such as dramatic style, cinematic technique, and theme or meaning are the exclusive domain of the director, and no one else. Andrew Sarris, a leading proponent of the auteur theory, defines the theory this way:

The first premise of the *auteur* theory is the technical competence of a director as a criterion of value. . . . The second premise . . . is the distinguishable personality of the director as a criterion of value. . . .

The third and ultimate premise . . . is concerned with interior meaning. . . . Interior meaning is extapolated from the tension between a director's personality and his material.[2]

In the case of Goldwyn's films, however, it is a stronger argument to suggest that Goldwyn, the first producer-auteur, was the one person responsible for the film, that, by maintaining tight control over all aspects of a production, Goldwyn provided the technique, style, and meaning to his films. The criterion for a Goldwyn film's evaluation becomes this: suppose Y instead of X has directed, would the film still be close to what it was? Suppose someone instead of Goldwyn had produced, would the film still be the same? The consistent use of key themes in films involving numerous writers and directors marks the individual films as genuinely Goldwyn products.

Richard Griffith has noted that Goldwyn's artistic control can be best revealed by means of deduction. In other words, true authorship of a film should be clear to any viewer who enters the theater. It is not the screen credits which define the creator's trademark, but rather the consistent and clearly individualistic style and values revealed in the film itself. In Goldwyn's films, this is the Goldwyn touch.[3]

Goldwyn's particular method was, in some senses, simple and easily duplicated. He started with good writing and high standards. He spent whatever money was necessary to achieve the effects he wanted.

The method, however, is difficult to execute in one particular area. Goldwyn maintained one-man control over all facets of production. He took the best advantage possible of the talents of those in his employ, but he was quick to override them when he thought it necessary. He worked closely with this camera operators and his directors. Despite his many fights, it was always Goldwyn who prevailed. If a director showed Goldwyn the "rushes" from a day's shooting and what Goldwyn saw did not match precisely his own visual conception of how the scenes should look, he would order the director to shoot the scenes over until they were to

Goldwyn's liking. Similarly, and more frequently done, if a script seemed weak or off the mark, Goldwyn would hound the writer for revisions. Sometimes this resulted in twenty different screenplays for the same film.

Perhaps Teresa Wright's comments on Goldwyn are typical of how his stars viewed that sort of control. "He was a true producer, seeing personally not only to the casting, but also to who would do the sets and who would create the costumes and even who the hairdresser would be. I found that he would comment on nearly everything I wore in the films I made for him, and he'd come in and sit for a while and tell the hairdresser exactly how my hair should be done. Curiously, he always had my hair lightened, and I thought 'What a crazy man. He hires brunettes and then dyes their hair.' He did it with me and with Merle Oberon and, I'm sure, with lots of others. I later found out the reason . . . ; dark hair photographs [on black and white film] jet black."[4]

Such total control today is, indeed, gone; there is even considerably less studio control over certain films than there was in Goldwyn's days.

Goldwyn's control, the Goldwyn touch, was Goldwyn's alone. He established no real tradition. A cinematic tradition consists of touches capable of being duplicated by others. The reason that there are no Goldwyn cinematic descendants is that he had an economic control which led to total artistic control. Having total artistic control meant that he could fashion his material to his own vision. That the emphasis in the Goldwyn touch was as much on the "Goldwyn" as it was on the "touch" was not obvious at the time.

It is at a distance that the importance of independence becomes clear: the independence he had as a producer serves not only as a metaphor for the emphasis he placed on human freedom but, more literally, as the source of his success. It is only when a producer has such independence, and has the willingness to spend the money when needed, and has an artistic vision to impart, that the film community and the film audience will find the next Goldwyn.

Samuel Goldwyn's name is not as famous as it once was, but, in time, his films will emerge as the unique and significant contributions they were.

"Samuel Goldwyn Presents" remains a trademark of a unified series of quality and humane films.

Notes and References

Chapter One

1. Samuel Goldwyn, "The Best Advice I Ever Had," *Reader's Digest*, June, 1956, p. 76.
2. Arthur Marx, *Goldwyn: A Biography of the Man Behind the Myth* (New York, 1976), p. 23.
3. Richard Griffith, *Samuel Goldwyn: The Producer and His Films* (New York, 1956), p. 9.
4. Marx, p. 102.
5. Ibid., p. 117.

Chapter Two

1. "Potash and Perlmutter," *New York Times*, September 24, 1923, p. 5.
2. "Bulldog Drummond," *New York Times*, May 3, 1929, p. 23.

Chapter Three

1. Alvin H. Marill, *Samuel Goldwyn Presents* (New York, 1976), p. 163.

Chapter Four

1. Mordaunt Hall, "*Street Scene*," *New York Times*, August 27, 1931, p. 22.
2. Marx, p. 250.
3. Griffith, p. 30.
4. Marx, p. 251.
5. Ibid., pp. 294–95.
6. Marill, p. 230.
7. Bosley Crowther, "*The North Star*," *New York Times*, November 5, 1943, p. 23.
8. Marill, p. 231.

Chapter Five

1. Marill, pp. 113–14.
2. Ibid., p. 114.

    3. Ibid., p. 114.
    4. Griffith, p. 25.
    5. Marx, p. 194.
    6. Marill, p. 135.
    7. Ibid.
    8. Mordaunt Hall, "*Nana*," *New York Times*, February 2, 1934, p. 20.
    9. Marill, p. 135.
   10. Ibid.
   11. Marx, p. 219.
   12. Frank S. Nugent, "*Dodsworth*," *New York Times*, September 24, 1936, p. 29.
   13. Marx, p. 263.
   14. Ibid., p. 263.
   15. Griffith, p. 33.
   16. Marx, p. 264.
   17. Griffith, p. 34.
   18. Frank S. Nugent, "*Wuthering Heights*," *New York Times*, April 14, 1939, p. 28.
   19. Marill, p. 149.
   20. Marx, p. 280.

Chapter Six

    1. Griffith, p. 39.
    2. Marill, p. 95.
    3. Ibid.
    4. Ibid., p. 94.
    5. Marx, p. 167.
    6. Marill, p. 172.
    7. Griffith, p. 23.
    8. Ibid., p. 31.
    9. Ibid.
   10. Marill, p. 176.
   11. Griffith, p. 31.
   12. Arthur Knight, *The Liveliest Art* (New York: Mentor Books, 1957), pp. 154–55.
   13. Marx, p. 260.
   14. Marill, p. 189.
   15. Ibid., p. 221.
   16. Ibid., p. 227.
   17. Marx, p. 301.
   18. Marill, p. 234.
   19. Ibid., p. 284.
   20. Ibid.
   21. Ibid., p. 288.

22. Marx, p. 343.

23. Bosley Crowther, *"Porgy and Bess,"* *New York Times*, January 25, 1959, p. 20.

Chapter Seven

1. Marx, p. 225.

2. Marill, p. 169.

3. Ibid., p. 213.

4. Ibid., p. 224.

5. Marx, p. 307.

6. Ibid., p. 308.

7. Griffith, p. 38.

8. Bosley Crowther, *"The Best Years of Our Lives,"* *New York Times*, November 22, 1946, p. 27.

9. Lewis Herman, *A Practical Manual of Screen Playwrighting* (Cleveland: World Publishing Company, 1963), p. 257.

10. Griffith, p. 41.

11. Ibid.

12. Marx, p. 316.

13. Knight, p. 245.

Chapter Eight

1. Marill, p. 7.

2. Andrew Sarris, *The Primal Screen: Essays on Film and Related Subjects* (New York, 1973), pp. 50–51.

3. Griffith, p. 5.

4. Marill, p. 7.

Selected Bibliography

1. Books

AGATE, JAMES. *Around Cinemas*. New York: Arno Press, 1972. A well-known critic's collected reviews including some of Goldwyn's work.

AGEE, JAMES. *Agee on Film: Volume One*. New York: Grossett & Dunlap, 1967. A collection of reviews mostly from *The Nation* including extended praise for William Wyler's and Gregg Toland's roles in *The Best Years of Our Lives*.

BLUESTONE, GEORGE. *Novels into Film*. Berkeley: University of California Press, 1961. This collection of brilliant essays concerning the relationship of novels and film contains an illuminating chapter on the similarities and differences in the literary and cinematic forms of *Wuthering Heights*.

CROWTHER, BOSLEY. *The Lion's Share: The Story of an Entertainment Empire*. New York: E. P. Dutton, 1957. This book relates the story of Metro-Goldwyn-Mayer and contains a lengthy chapter on Goldwyn's part in the business end of the company.

DEMILLE, CECIL B. *Autobiography*. Edited by Donald Hayne. Englewood Cliffs, N.J.: Prentice-Hall, 1959. The not-always friendly relations between DeMille and Goldwyn are described in useful biographical detail.

EASTON, CAROL. *The Search for Sam Goldwyn: A Biography*. New York: Wm. Morrow, 1976. This is an odd attack on Goldwyn, seemingly undertaken as a personal vendetta. The book is full of embarrassing anecdotes, and contains neither useful information nor analysis.

FARRAR, GERALDINE. *Such Sweet Compulsion*. New York: Greystone Press, 1938. The sixth chapter of this autobiography of an actress is devoted to an insightful account of working with Goldwyn.

FERGUSON, OTIS. *The Film Criticism of Otis Ferguson*. Edited by Robert Wilson. Philadelphia: Temple University Press, 1971. A collection of essays, a number of which touch on Goldwyn's films, especially *Dead End* and *The Wedding Night*.

FRENCH, PHILIP. *The Movie Moguls: An Informal History of the Hollywood Tycoons*. Chicago: Regnery, 1969. The brief material on Goldwyn is concentrated on his shortcomings, but provides an interesting analysis of the relationship between Goldwyn and his audience.

GOLDWYN, SAMUEL. *Behind the Screen.* New York: George H. Doran, 1923. This is a ghost-written, chatty autobiography about Goldwyn's love of the people in the film industry, but contains very little information about his past or even the current life.

GREENE, GRAHAM. *Graham Greene on Film: Collected Film Criticism 1935–1940.* Edited by John Russell Taylor. New York: Simon & Schuster, 1972. A large selection of reviews including many of Goldwyn films—most notably the insightful reviews of *Dodsworth* and *Dead End.*

GRIFFITH, RICHARD. *Samuel Goldwyn: The Producer and His Films.* New York: Museum of Modern Art Film Library, 1956. This is a ground-breaking, but unfortunately brief, analysis of Goldwyn's contributions. Careful analysis is provided for almost all of the important films.

HECHT, BEN. "Enter the Movies." In *Film: An Anthology,* edited by Daniel Talbot, pp. 257–87. Berkeley: University of California Press, 1966. This essay is a contentious discussion of the role of screenplay writer. Hecht's work with Goldwyn is mentioned in a rare positive moment.

JOHNSTON, ALVA. *The Great Goldwyn.* New York: Random House, 1937. The book contains essays originally published in the *Saturday Evening Post,* which contain interesting anecdotal material for popular biographies but fail to uncover the creative artist.

LASKY, JESSE L., with DON WELDON. *I Blow My Own Horn.* Garden City, N.Y.: Doubleday, 1957. Goldwyn's first partner, and ex-brother-in-law, tells his side of their partnership and breakup.

MARILL, ALVIN H. *Samuel Goldwyn Presents.* New York: A. S. Barnes, 1976. This is a large-size pictorial review of all of Goldwyn's films providing credits, production stories, and excerpts from reviews. There is no analysis of the individual films.

MARX, ARTHUR. *Goldwyn: A Biography of the Man Behind the Myth.* New York: Norton, 1976. A full-length study which is often humorous and frequently useful in detailing accounts of particular productions. The book concentrates on Goldwynisms and the movie industry without providing any aesthetic analysis of the films.

SARRIS, ANDREW. *The Primal Screen: Essays on Film and Related Subjects.* New York: Simon & Schuster, 1973. Three of this collection of essays explicitly discuss the auteur theory.

WARSHOW, ROBERT. *The Immediate Experience: Movies, Comics, Theatre, and Other Aspects of Popular Culture.* New York: Atheneum, 1972. The essays in this book contain an interesting analysis of film's place in our culture, and a well-known attack on *The Best Years of Our Lives.*

WYLER, WILLIAM, and MADSEN, AXEL. *William Wyler.* New York: Thomas Y. Crowell, 1973. Wyler's stormy encounters with Goldwyn are retold without adding new information but from an insider's view, especially useful on *The Best Years of Our Lives.*

ZIEROLD, NORMAN. *The Moguls*. New York: Coward-McCann & Geoghe-
    gan, 1969. These biographical essays, which are essentially anecdotal
    provide overviews of Goldwyn and his contemporaries.

2. Articles

BRANDT, CARL. "The Celluloid Prince." *New York*, April 25, 1925, pp. 13–
    14. A discussion by Goldwyn's press agent of Goldwyn's aesthetics and
    the relation between what he strives for and what he achieves. The
    tone alternates between praise and criticism. On balance it is an
    unflattering portrait.

BUTTERFIELD, ROGER. "Sam Goldwyn." *Life*, October 17, 1947, pp. 126–
    142. A broad review of Goldwyn's career, but without new information.

CROWTHER, BOSLEY. "*The Best Years of Our Lives.*" *New York Times*,
    November 22, 1946, p. 27. An important review in which Goldwyn's
    triumphant film is considered "not only . . . superlative entertainment
    but . . . food for quiet and humanizing thought." (Collected in *The
    New York Times Film Reviews*, 3:2146–47.)

FRENCH, PHILIP. "Star Struck." *New Statesman*, October 8, 1976, pp. 485–
    86. This is a review of Arthur Marx's biography of Goldwyn. French is
    critical of the notion that Goldwyn was an artist and an innovator.

GOLDWYN, FRANCES. "Dear Sam: Do you Remember?" *Woman's Home
    Companion*, December, 1950, pp. 42–44. The second Mrs. Goldwyn
    provides a nostalgic reminiscence which imparts affection. Frances
    Goldwyn was a devoted wife and confident helper, qualities which
    come through.

GOLDWYN, SAM. "The Best Advice I Ever Had." *Reader's Digest*, June,
    1956, pp. 75–77. A ghost-written account of advice Goldwyn got as a
    nine-year-old child in Warsaw, the essence of which was that "darkness
    can be overcome."

LUFT, HERBERT G. "Samuel Goldwyn." *Films in Review*, December, 1969,
    pp. 585–604. A brief review of Goldwyn's life and films that is
    substantially a filmography.

LYON, PETER. "The Hollywood Picture: A Script." *Hollywood Quarterly*,
    Summer, 1948, pp. 341–61. This is a fascinating transcript of a
    November 3, 1948, radio broadcast on CBS about the making of *The
    Best Years of Our Lives*.

WILSON, EDMUND. "It's Terrible! It's Ghastly! It Stinks!" *New Republic*,
    November 22, 1954, pp. 72–74. A discussion of Alva Johnston's
    biography in which Wilson argues that Goldwyn's films are false and
    vulgar. (This is a reprint of a July 21, 1937, column in *New Republic*.)

Filmography

Because of the large number of films produced by Samuel Goldwyn, some of only ephemeral interest, the entries in this filmography are shorter than those in most other books of this series. Since all the films listed were produced by Goldwyn Productions, this name is not repeated in each entry. The release date of the film follows the title parenthetically; the running time is given where known. Only the names of the principal director, scriptwriter(s), cinematographer, and composer(s) of the musical score are given along with the sources of the screenplay and a list of principal members of the cast. Since virtually all of Samuel Goldwyn's talking pictures since *One Heavenly Night* (1931) are available for 16mm. noncommercial rental from MacMillan/Audio Brandon, 34 MacQueston Parkway South, Mount Vernon, New York, at the time of this writing, separate information is not given for each film. Some films are for rent or sale from other sources as well, but Samuel Goldwyn 16 originally planned as an outlet for these films has ceased operations. For further details consult the current edition of James Limbacher's *Feature Films for Rent or Sale on 8mm. and 16mm.* More detailed information about some of Goldwyn's most important productions may be found in *William Wyler* by Michael Anderegg (Twayne, 1979).

The Editor

THE ETERNAL CITY (1923)
Director: George Fitzmaurice
Screenplay: Ouida Bergere, from the story by Sir Hall Caine
Music: Luigi Giuffrida, Kitty McLoughlin
Cast: Lionel Barrymore (Baron Bonelli), Bert Lytell (David Rossi), Barbara
    La Marr (Roma), Richard Bennett (Bruno)
Premiere: January 20, 1924, Strand Theater, New York

POTASH AND PERLMUTTER (1923)
Director: Clarence Badger

177

Screenplay: Frances Marion, from the play by Montague Glass and Charles
    Stein
Cinematographer: Rudolph Berquist
Music: Mark Strand Symphony Orchestra
Case: Barney Bernard (Abe Potash), Alexander Carr (Morris Perlmutter),
    Vera Gordon (Rosie Potash), Martha Mansfield (Head Model), Ben
    Lyon (Boris Andrieff)
Premiere: September 6, 1923, Rivoli Theater, Baltimore, Md.

CYTHEREA (1924)
Director: George Fitzmaurice
Screenplay: Frances Marion, from the novel by Joseph Hergesheimer
Cinematographer: Arthur Miller
Editor: Stuart Heisler
Cast: Lewis Stone (Lee Randon), Constance Bennett (Annette Sherwin),
    Irene Rich (Fanny Randon), Alma Rubens (Savina Grove), Norman
    Kerry (Peyton Morris)
Premiere: May 25, 1924, Strand Theater, New York

IN HOLLYWOOD WITH POTASH AND PERLMUTTER (1924)
Director: Al Green
Screenplay: Frances Marion, from the play by Montague Glass and Jules
    Eckert Goodman
Cinematographers: Arthur Miller and Harry Hollenberger
Cast: Alexander Carr (Morris Perlmutter), George Sidney (Abe Potash),
    Norma and Constance Talmadge (as themselves), Betty Blythe (Rita
    Sismondi), Vera Gordon (Rosie Potash)
Premiere: September 29, 1924, Strand Theater, New York

TARNISH (1924)
Director: George Fitzmaurice
Screenplay: Frances Marion, from the play by Gilbert Emery
Cinematographers: Arthur Miller and Billy Tuers
Cast: Ronald Colman (Emmett Carr), May McAvoy (Letitia Tevis), Marie
    Prevost (Nettie Dark), Albert Gran (Adolf Tevis), Norman Kerry (Johon
    Graves), Harry Myers (The Barber)
Premiere: October 12, 1924, Strand Theater, New York

A THIEF IN PARADISE (1925)
Director: George Fitzmaurice
Screenplay: Frances Marion, from the novel *The Worldlings* by Leonard
    Merrick

Cinematographer: Arthur Miller

Cast: Doris Kenyon (Helen Saville), Ronald Colman (Maurice Blake), Aileen Pringle (Rosa), Claude Gillingwater (Jardin), Alec Francis (Bishop Saville), John Patrick (Ned Whelan)

Premiere: January 25, 1925, Strand Theater, New York

HIS SUPREME MOMENT (1925)

Director: George Fitzmaurice

Screenplay: Frances Marion, from the novel *World Without End* by May Edington

Cinematographer: Arthur Miller

Cast: Blanche Sweet (Carla King), Ronald Colman (John Douglas), Kathleen Myers (Sara Deeping) Belle Bennett (Carla Light)

Premiere: April 12, 1925, Strand Theater, New York

THE DARK ANGEL (1925)

Director: George Fitzmaurice

Screenplay: Frances Marion, from the play by H. B. Trevelyan (Guy Bolton)

Cinematographer: George Barnes

Cast: Vilma Banky (Kitty Vane), Ronald Colman (Captain Hilary Trent), Helen Jerome Eddy (Miss Bottles), Wyndham Standing (Gerald Shannon), Frank Elliot (Lord Beaumont)

Premiere: October 11, 1925, Strand Theater, New York

STELLA DALLAS (1925)

Director: Henry King

Screenplay: Frances Marion, from the novel by Olive Higgins Prouty

Cinematographer: Arthur Edeson

Cast: Ronald Colman (Stephen Dallas), Belle Bennett (Stella Dallas), Lois Moran (Laurel Dallas), Alice Joyce (Helen Morrison), Douglas Fairbanks, Jr. (Richard Grosvenor), Jean Hersholt (Ed Munn)

Premiere: November 16, 1925, Apollo Theater, New York

PARTNERS AGAIN (1926)

Director: Henry King

Screenplay: Frances Marion, from the play by Montague Glass and Jules Eckert Goodman

Cinematographer: Arthur Edeson

Cast: Alexander Carr (Morris Perlmutter), George Sidney (Abe Potash), Betty Jewel (Hattie Potash), Allan Forrest (Don), Robert Schable

(Schenckmann), Gilbert Clayton (Mr. Sammett), Lillian Elliot (Rosie Potash)
Premiere: February 14, 1926, Strand Theater, New York

THE WINNING OF BARBARA WORTH (1926)
Director: Henry King
Screenplay: Frances Marion, from the novel by Harold Bell
Cinematographers: George Barnes and Gregg Toland
Cast: Ronald Colman (Willard Holmes), Vilma Banky (Barbara Worth), Gary Cooper (Abe Lee), Charles Lane (Jefferson Worth), Paul McAllister (the Seer), Sam Blum (Blanton)
Premiere: October 14, 1926, Forum Theater, Los Angeles

THE NIGHT OF LOVE (1927)
Director: George Fitzmaurice
Screenplay: Lenore Coffee, from a story by Pedro Calderon de la Barca
Cinematographers: George Barnes and Thomas E. Brannigan
Cast: Ronald Colman (Montero), Vilma Banky (Princess Marie), Montague Love (Duke Bernardo de la Gorda), Natalie Kingston (Donna Beatriz), Laska Winter (Gypsy Bride), Sally Rand (Gypsy Dancer), John George (Jester)
Premiere: January 24, 1927, Strand Theater, New York

THE MAGIC FLAME (1927)
Director: Henry King
Screenplay: Adapted by Bess Meredyth from Rudolph Lothar's play *King Harlequin*
Cinematographer: George Barnes
Cast: Ronald Colman (Tito/Count Casati), Vilma Banky (Bianca), Augustino Borgato (Ringmaster)
Premiere: September 18, 1927, Strand Theater, New York

THE DEVIL DANCER (1927)
Director: Fred Niblo
Screenplay: Adapted by Alice D. G. Miller from a story by Harry Hervey
Cinematographers: George Barnes and Thomas Brannigan
Cast: Gilda Gray (Talka), Clive Brook (Stephen Athelstan), Anna May Wong (Sada)
Premiere: December 18, 1927, Rivoli Theater, New York

TWO LOVERS (1928)
Director: Fred Niblo
Screenplay: Adapted by Alice D. G. Miller from Baroness Orczy's novel
    Leatherface
Cinematographer: George Barnes
Art Director: Carl Oscar Borg
Music: Hugo Riesenfeld
Editor: Viola Lawrence
Cast: Ronald Colman (Mark Van Ryke), Vilma Banky (Oonna Lenora de
    Vargas), Noah Beery (Duke of Azar)
Premiere: March 22, 1928, Embassy Theater, New York

THE AWAKENING (1928)
Director: Victor Fleming
Screenplay: Carey Wilson, based on a story by Frances Marion
Cinematographer: George Barnes
Music: Hugo Riesenfeld; the song "Marie" by Irving Berlin
Cast: Vilma Banky (Marie), Walter Byron (Count Karl von Hagen), Louis
    Wolheim (La Bete)
Running Time: 100 minutes
Premiere: December 30, 1928, Rivoli Theater, New York

THE RESCUE (1929)
Director: Herbert Brenon
Assistant Director: Roy Lissner
Screenplay: Adapted by Elizabeth Meehan from the story by Joseph Conrad
Cinematographer: George Barnes
Music: Hugo Riesenfeld
Cast: Ronald Colman (Tom Lingard), Lily Damita (Edith Travers), Theo-
    dore von Eltz (Carter)
Running Time: 96 minutes
Premiere: January 13, 1929, Rialto Theater, New York

BULLDOG DRUMMOND (1929)
Director: F. Richard Jones
Screenplay: Sidney Howard and Wallace Smith, based on the novel by
    Herman McNeile and the play by McNeile and Gerald DuMaurier
Cinematographers: George Barnes and Gregg Toland
Cast: Ronald Colman (Hugo "Bulldog" Drummond), Joan Bennett (Phyllis
    Benton), Lilyan Tashman (Erma), Montague Love (Peterson)
Running Time: 80 minutes
Premiere: May 2, 1929, Apollo Theater, New York

THIS IS HEAVEN (1929)
Director: Al Santell
Screenplay: Adapted by Hope Loring from a story by Arthur Mantell
Cinematographers: George Barnes and Gregg Toland
Music: Hugo Riesenfeld; title song by Jack Yellin and Harry Akst
Cast: Vilma Banky (Eva Petrie), James Hall (James Stackpole), Luciene
    Littlefield (Frank Chase), Fritzie Ridgeway (Mamie Chase)
Running Time: 90 minutes
Premiere: May 26, 1929, Rivoli Theater, New York

CONDEMNED (1929)
Director: Wesley Ruggles
Screenplay: Adapted by Sidney Howard from the novel *Condemned to
    Devil's Island* by Blair Niles
Cinematographers: George Barnes and Gregg Toland
Cast: Ronald Colman (Michael Oban), Ann Harding (Mme. Vidal), Louis
    Wolheim (Jacques Duval)
Running Time: 93 minutes
Premiere: November 3, 1929, Selwyn Theater, New York

RAFFLES (1930)
Directors: Harry D'Arrast and George Fitzmaurice
Screenplay: Adapted by Sidney Howard from E. W. Hornung's stories
    "The Amateur Cracksman"
Cinematographers: George Barnes and Gregg Toland
Cast: Ronald Colman (Raffles), Kay Francis (Lady Gwen), Bramwell
    Fletcher (Bunny Manders), Francis Dade (Ethel Crowley)
Running Time: 70 minutes
Premiere: July 24, 1930, Rialto Theater, New York

WHOOPEE! (1930)
Director: Thornton Freeland
Coproducer: Florenz Ziegfeld
Screenplay: Adapted by William Conselman from the comedy by William
    Anthony McGuire
Cinematographers: Lee Garmes, Ray Renahan, Gregg Toland
Music: Alfred Newman
Cast: Eddie Cantor (Henry Williams), Eleanor Hunt (Sally Morgan), Paul
    Gregory (Wanenis)
Running Time: 85 minutes
Premiere: October 1, 1930, Rivoli Theater, New York

THE DEVIL TO PAY (1930)
Director: George Fitzmaurice
Screenplay: Adapted by Benjamin Glazer from Frederick Lonsdale's screen-
play
Cinematographers: George Barnes and Gregg Toland
Cast: Ronald Colman (Willie Leeland), Loretta Young (Dorothy Hope),
Florence Britton (Susan Leeland)
Running Time: 72 minutes
Premiere: December 18, 1930, Gaiety Theater, New York

ONE HEAVENLY NIGHT (1931)
Director: George Fitzmaurice
Screenplay: Adapted by Sidney Howard, based on a story by Louis
Bromfield
Cinematographers: George Barnes and Gregg Toland
Cast: Evelyn Laye (Lilli), John Boles (Count Mirko Tibor), Leon Errol
(Otto)
Running Time: 82 minutes
Premiere: January 9, 1931, Rialto Theater, New York

STREET SCENE (1931)
Director: King Vidor
Screenplay: Adapted by Elmer Rice from his play
Cinematographer: George Barnes
Music: Alfred Newman
Cast: Sylvia Sidney (Rose Maurrant), Wm. Collier, Jr. (Samuel Kaplan),
Estelle Taylor (Anna Maurrant)
Running Time: 82 minutes
Premiere: August 26, 1931, Rivoli Theater, New York

PALMY DAYS (1931)
Director: A. Edward Sutherland
Screenplay: Eddie Cantor, Morris Ryskind, David Freedman, Keene
Thompson
Cinematographer: Gregg Toland
Music: Afred Newman; choreography by Busby Berkeley
Cast: Eddie Cantor (Eddie Simpson), Charlotte Greenwood (Helen Martin),
Barbara Weeks (Joan Clark), George Raft (Joe the Frog)
Running Time: 77 minutes
Premiere: September 23, 1931, Rialto Theater, New York

THE UNHOLY GARDEN (1931)
Director: George Fitzmaurice
Screenplay: Ben Hecht and Charles MacArthur
Cinematographers: George Barnes and Gregg Toland
Music: Alfred Newman
Cast: Ronald Colman (Barrington Hent), Fay Wray (Camille), Estelle
    Taylor (Elise Mowbry)
Running Time: 75 minutes
Premiere: October 28, 1931, Rialto Theater, New York

ARROWSMITH (1931)
Director: John D. Ford
Screenplay: Sidney Howard, from the novel by Sinclair Lewis
Cinematographer: Ray June
Music: Alfred Newman
Cast: Ronald Colman (Martin Arrowsmith), Richard Bennett (Sondelius),
    Helen Hayes (Leora), Myrna Loy (Joyce Lanyon)
Running Time: 112 minutes
Premiere: December 7, 1931, Gaiety Theater, New York

TONIGHT OR NEVER (1931)
Director: Mervyn Le Roy
Screenplay: Adapted by Ernest Vajda from the play by Lily Hatvany
Cinematographer: Gregg Toland
Music: Alfred Newman
Cast: Gloria Swanson (Mella Vego), Ferdinand Gottschalk (Rudig), Robert
    Gregg (the Butler), Melvyn Douglas (Jim)
Running Time: 66 minutes
Premiere: December 17, 1931, Rialto Theater, New York

THE GREEKS HAD A WORD FOR THEM (1932)
Rereleased as **THOSE BROADWAY GIRLS**
Director: Lowell Sherman
Screenplay: Sidney Howard, from the play by Zoe Alcin
Cinematographer: George Barnes
Music: Afred Newman
Cast: Ina Claire (Jean Lawrence), Madge Evans (Polaire), Joan Blondell
    (Schatze), David Manners (Emery)
Running Time: 77 minutes
Premiere: February 3, 1932, Rialto Theater, New York

THE KID FROM SPAIN (1932)

Director: Leo McCarey

Screenplay: William Anthony McGuire, Bert Kalmar, and Harry Ruby

Cinematographer: Gregg Toland

Music: Alfred Newman; dances staged by Busby Berkeley; music and lyrics by Bert Kalmer and Harry Ruby

Cast: Eddie Cantor (Eddie Williams), Lyda Roberti (Rosalie), Robert Young (Ricardo)

Running Time: 96 minutes

Premiere: November 17, 1932, Palace Theater, New York

CYNARA (1932)

Director: King Vidor

Screenplay: Adapted by Frances Marion and Lynn Starling from the play by H. M. Harwood and Robert Gore-Brown, based on Gore-Brown's novel *An Imperfect Lover*

Cinematographer: Ray June

Music: Alfred Newman

Cast: Ronald Colman (Jim Warlock), Kay Francis (Clemency Warlock), Phyllis Barry (Doris Lea)

Running Time: 78 minutes

Premiere: December 24, 1932, Rivoli Theater, New York

THE MASQUERADER (1933)

Director: Richard Wallace

Screenplay: Adapted by Howard Estabrook from the story by Katherine Cecil Thurston and John Hunter Booth; dialogue by Moss Hart

Cinematographer: Gregg Toland

Music: Alfred Newman

Cast: Ronald Colman (Sir John Chilcote/John Loder), Elissa Landi (Eva Chilcote), Juliette Compton (Lady Joyce)

Running Time: 78 minutes

Premiere: September 3, 1933, Rivoli Theater, New York

ROMAN SCANDALS (1933)

Director: Frank Tuttle

Screenplay: Adapted by William Anthony McGuire and George Oppenheimer from the play by George S. Kaufman and Robert Sherwood

Cinematographer: Gregg Toland

Music: Alfred Newman; dances staged by Busby Berkeley

Cast: Eddie Cantor (Eddie), Gloria Stuart (Princess Sylvia), Ruth Etting (Olga)

Running Time: 92 minutes
Premiere: December 25, 1933, Rivoli Theater, New York

NANA (1934)

Director: Dorothy Arzner
Screenplay: Willard Mack and Harry Wagstaff Gribble, suggested by the
    novel by Emile Zola
Cinematographer: Gregg Toland
Music: Alfred Newman; song "That's Love" by Richard Rodgers and
    Lorenz Hart
Cast: Anna Sten (Nana), Lionel Atwill (Colonel Andre Muffat), Phillips
    Holmes (Lieutenant George Muffat), Richard Bennett (Gaston Greiner)
Running Time: 87 minutes
Premiere: February 1, 1934, Radio City Music Hall, New York

WE LIVE AGAIN (1934)

Director: Rouben Mamoulian
Screenplay: Adapted by Preston Sturges, Maxwell Anderson, and Leonard
    Praskins from Leo Tolstoy's novel *Resurrection*
Cinematographer: Gregg Toland
Music: Alfred Newman
Cast: Anna Sten (Katusha Maslova), Jane Baxter (Missy Kortchagin),
    Frederic March (Prince Dmitri Nekhlyudov), C. Aubrey Smith (Prince
    Kort)
Running Time: 85 minutes
Premiere: November 1, 1934, Radio City Music Hall, New York

KID MILLIONS (1934)

Director: Roy Del Ruth
Screenplay: Arthur Sheekman, Nat Perrin, and Nunnally Johnson
Cinematographer: Ray June
Music: Alfred Newman; songs by Walter Donaldson and Gus Kahn, Burton
    Lane and Harold Adamson, and Irving Berlin; dances by Seymour
    Felix
Cast: Eddie Cantor (Eddie), Ann Sothern (Jane Larrabee), Ethel Merman
    (Dot), George Murphy (Jerry Lane)
Running Time: 90 minutes
Premiere: November 11, 1934, Rivoli Theater, New York

THE WEDDING NIGHT (1935)

Director: King Vidor
Screenplay: Edwin Knopf; scenario by Ruth Fitzgerald

Cinematographer: Gregg Toland
Music: Alfred Newman
Cast: Anna Sten (Manya Novak), Gary Cooper (Tony Barrett), Helen
    Vinson (Dora), Ralph Bellamy (Frederik Sobieski)
Running Time: 81 minutes
Premiere: March 16, 1935, Rivoli Theater, New York

THE DARK ANGEL (1935)
Director: Sidney Franklin
Screenplay: Lillian Hellman and Mordaunt Shairp, based on the play by
    H.B. Trevelyan (Guy Bolton)
Cinematographer: Gregg Toland
Music: Alfred Newman
Cast: Frederic March (Alan Trent), Herbert Marshall (Gerald Shannon),
    Merle Oberon (Kitty Vane)
Running Time: 105 minutes
Premiere: September 5, 1935, Rivoli Theater, New York

BARBARY COAST (1935)
Rereleased as **PORT OF WICKEDNESS**
Director: Howard Hawks
Screenplay: Charles MacArthur and Ben Hecht
Cinematographer: Ray June
Music: Alfred Newman
Cast: Miriam Hopkins (Mary Rutledge), Joel McCrea (James Carmichael),
    Edward G. Robinson (Louis Chamalis), Walter Brennan (Old Atrocity)
Running Time: 90 minutes
Premiere: October 13, 1935, Rivoli Theater, New York

SPLENDOR (1935)
Director: Elliott Nugent
Screenplay: Rachel Crothers
Cinematographer: Gregg Toland
Music: Alfred Newman
Cast: Miriam Hopkins (Phyllis Lorrimore), Paul Cavanaugh (Martin Deer-
    ing), Joel McCrea (Brighton Lorrimore), Helen Westley (Mrs. Lorri-
    more)
Running Time: 77 minutes
Premiere: November 22, 1935, Rivoli Theater, New York

STRIKE ME PINK (1936)
Director: Norman Taurog
Screenplay: Adapted by Frank Butler, Walter De Leon, Francis Martin, and Philip Rapp from Clarence Buddington Kelland's story, "Dreamland"
Cinematographers: Gregg Toland and Merritt Gerstad
Music: Alfred Newman; music and lyrics by Harold Arlen and Lew Brown
Cast: Eddit Cantor (Eddie Pink), Ethel Merman (Joyce Lenox), Sally Eilers (Claribel Hayes)
Running Time: 100 minutes
Premiere: January 17, 1936, Radio City Music Hall, New York

THESE THREE (1936)
Director: William Wyler
Screenplay: Lillian Hellman, based on her play *The Children's Hour*
Cinematographer: Gregg Toland
Music: Alfred Newman
Cast: Miriam Hopkins (Martha Dobie), Merle Oberon (Karen Wright), Joel McCrea (Dr. Joseph Cardin), Catherine Doucet (Mrs. Mortar)
Running Time: 92 minutes
Premiere: March 18, 1936, Rivoli Theater, New York

DODSWORTH (1936)
Director: William Wyler
Screenplay: Adapted by Sidney Howard from his own play and the novel by Sinclair Lewis
Cinematographer: Rudolph Maté
Music: Alfred Newman
Cast: Walter Huston (Samuel Dodsworth), Ruth Chatterton (Fran Dodsworth), Mary Astor (Edith Cortright), Paul Lukas (Arnold Iselin), David Niven (Clyde Lockert), Gregory Gaye (Kurt Von Obersdorf), Maria Ouspenskaya (Baroness Von Obersdorf)
Running Time: 101 minutes
Premiere: September 23, 1936, Rivoli Theater, New York

COME AND GET IT (1936)
Rereleased as **ROARING TIMBER**
Directors: Howard Hawks and William Wyler
Screenplay: Adapted by Jules Furthman and Jan Murfin from the novel by Edna Ferber
Cinematographers: Gregg Toland and Rudolph Maté
Music: Alfred Newman
Cast: Edward Arnold (Barney Glasgow), Joel McCrea (Richard Glasgow),

Frances Farmer (Lotta Morgan/Lotta Bostrom), Walter Brennan (Swan Bostrom)
Running Time: 99 minutes
Premiere: November 11, 1936, Rivoli Theater, New York

BELOVED ENEMY (1936)

Director: H. C. Porter
Screenplay: John Balderston, Rose Franken, William Brown Meloney, and David Hart, from a story by John Balderston
Cinematographer: Gregg Toland
Music: Alfred Newman
Cast: Merle Oberon (Helen Drummond), Brian Aherne (Dennis Riordan), Karen Morley (Cathleen O'Brien), Henry Stephenson (Lord Athleigh)
Running Time: 90 minutes
Premiere: December 25, 1936, Rivoli Theater, New York

WOMAN CHASES MAN (1937)

Director: John G. Blystone
Screenplay: Joseph Anthony, Manuel Seff, and David Hertz, from the story by Lynn Root and Franklin Fenton
Cinematographer: Gregg Toland
Music: Alfred Newman
Cast: Miriam Hopkins (Virginia Travis), Joel McCrea (Kenneth Nolan), Charles Winninger (B. J. Nolan), Ella Logan (Judy Williams), Broderick Crawford (Hunk Williams)
Running Time: 71 minutes
Premiere: June 10, 1936, Radio City Music Hall, New York

STELLA DALLAS (1937)

Director: King Vidor
Screenplay: Adapted by Victor Heerman, Sara Y. Mason, and Harry Wagstaff Gribble from the novel by Olive Higgins Prouty
Cinematographer: Rudolph Maté
Music: Alfred Newman
Cast: Barbara Stanwyck (Stella Dallas), John Boles (Stephen Dallas), Anne Shirley (Laurel Dallas), Barbara O'Neil (Helen Morrison)
Running time: 106 minutes
Premiere: August 5, 1937, Radio City Music Hall, New York

DEAD END (1937)

Director: William Wyler
Screenplay: Lilliam Hellman, from Sidney Kingsley's play

Cinematographer: Gregg Toland
Music: Alfred Newman
Cast: Sylvia Sidney (Drina), Joel McCrea (Dave), Humphrey Bogart ("Baby Face" Martin), Wendy Barrie (Kay), Claire Trevor (Francey), and Billy Halop, Huntz Hall, Leo Gorcey, and Bobby Jordan as the "Dead End Kids"
Running Time: 92 minutes
Premiere: August 24, 1937, Rivoli Theater, New York

THE HURRICANE (1937)
Directors: John Ford and Stuart Heisler
Screenplay: Adapted by Oliver H. Garrett and Dudley Nichols from the novel by Charles Nordhoff and James Norman Hall
Cinematographer: Bert Glennon
Music: Alfred Newman
Cast: Dorothy Lamour (Marama), Jon Hall (Terengi), Mary Astor (Mme. De Laage), C. Aubrey Smith (Father Paul)
Running Time: 110 minutes
Premiere: November 9, 1937, Astor Theater, New York

THE GOLDWYN FOLLIES (1938)
Directors: George Marshall and H. C. Potter
Screenplay: Ben Hecht
Cinematographer: Gregg Toland
Music: Alfred Newman; music and lyrics by George and Ira Gershwin; additional music by Vernon Duke; ballet scenes directed by George Balanchine
Cast: Adolphe Menjou (Oliver Merlin), Zorina (Olga Samara), Andrea Leeds (Hazel Dawes), Kenny Baker (Danny Beecher)
Running Time: 115 minutes
Premiere: February 20, 1938, Rivoli Theater, New York

THE ADVENTURES OF MARCO POLO (1938)
Directors: Archie Mayo and John Ford
Screenplay: Adapted by Robert E. Sherwood from a story by N. A. Pogson
Cinematographers: Rudolph Maté and Archie Stout
Music: Alfred Newman; score by Hugo Friedhofer
Cast: Gary Cooper (Marco Polo), Sigrid Gurie (Princess Kukachin), Basil Rathbone (Ahmed), George Barbier (Kublai Khan)
Running Time: 104 minutes
Premiere: April 7, 1938, Radio City Music Hall, New York

THE COWBOY AND THE LADY (1938)

Director: Henry C. Potter

Screenplay: Adapted by S. N. Behrman and Sonya Levien from an original
 story by Leo McCarey and Frank R. Adams

Cinematographer: Gregg Toland

Music: Alfred Newman

Cast: Gary Cooper (Stretch Willoughby), Merle Oberon (Mary Smith),
 Patsy Kelly (Kate Callahan), Walter Brennan (Sugar)

Running Time: 91 minutes

Premiere: November 24, 1938, Radio City Music Hall, New York

WUTHERING HEIGHTS (1939)

Director: William Wyler

Screenplay: Ben Hecht and Charles MacArthur, from the Emily Brontë
 novel

Cinematographer: Gregg Toland

Music: Alfred Newman

Cast: Merle Oberon (Cathy Earnshaw), Laurence Olivier (Heathcliff),
 David Niven (Edgar Linton), Flora Robson (Ellen Dean), Donald Crisp
 (Dr. Kenneth)

Running Time: 104 minutes

Premiere: April 13, 1939, Rivoli Theater, New York

THEY SHALL HAVE MUSIC (1939)

Rereleased as **RAGGED ANGELS**

Director: Archie Mayo

Screenplay: Irmgard Von Cube and John Howard Lawson, from the novel
 by Charles L. Clifford

Cinematographer: Gregg Toland

Music: Alfred Newman

Cast: Jascha Heifetz (himself), Andrea Leeds (Ann Lawson), Joel McCrea
 (Peter), Walter Brennan (Professor Lawson)

Running Time: 102 minutes

Premiere: July 25, 1939, Rivoli Theater, New York

THE REAL GLORY (1939)

Director: Henry Hathaway

Screenplay: Adapted by Jo Swerling and Robert R. Presnell from the novel
 by Charles L. Clifford

Cinematographer: Rudolph Maté

Music: Alfred Newman

Cast: Gary Cooper (Doctor Bill Canavan), Andrea Leeds (Linda Hartley),
    David Niven (Lieutenant McCool), Reginald Owen (Captain Hartley)
Running Time: 96 minutes
Premiere: September 15, 1939, Rivoli Theater, New York

RAFFLES (1940)
Director: Sam Wood
Screenplay: Adapted by John Van Druten and Sidney Howard from E. W.
    Hornung's *The Amateur Cracksman*
Cinematographer: Gregg Toland
Music: Victor Young
Cast: David Niven (Raffles), Dame May Whitty (Lady Melrose), Dudley
    Digges (Mackenzie), Olivia De Havilland (Gwen)
Running Time: 71 minutes
Premiere: January 12, 1940, Roxy Theater, New York

THE WESTERNER (1940)
Director: William Wyler
Screenplay: Adapted by Jo Swerling and Niven Busch from the story by
    Stuary Lake
Cinematographer: Gregg Toland
Music: Dmitri Tiomkin
Cast: Gary Cooper (Cole Haren), Walter Brennan (Judge Roy Bean), Fred
    Stone (Caliphet Mathews)
Running Time: 100 minutes
Premiere: October 24, 1940, Radio City Music Hall, New York

THE LITTLE FOXES (1941)
Director: William Wyler
Screenplay: Lillian Hellman, with additional scenes and dialogue by
    Dorothy Parker, Arthur Kober, and Alan Campbell, from Lillian
    Hellman's play
Cinematographer: Gregg Toland
Music: Meredith Wilson
Cast: Bette Davis (Regina Giddens), Herbert Marshall (Horace Giddens),
    Teresa Wright (Alexandra Giddens), Richard Carlson (David Hewitt)
Running Time: 116 minutes
Premiere: August 21, 1941, Radio City Music Hall, New York

BALL OF FIRE (1941)
Director: Howard Hawks
Screenplay: Adapted by Billy Wilder and Charles Brackett from the story
    "From A to Z" by Billy Wilder and Thomas Monroe

Cinematographer: Gregg Toland
Music: Alfred Newman; song "Drum Boogie" by Gene Krupa and Ray Eldridge
Cast: Gary Cooper (Professor Bertram Potts), Barbara Stanwyck (Sugarpuss O'Shea), Oscar Homolka (Professor Gurkaroff), Dana Andrews (Joe Lilac)
Running Time: 111 minutes
Premiere: January 15, 1942, Radio City Music Hall, New York

THE PRIDE OF THE YANKEES (1942)

Director: Sam Wood
Screenplay: Adapted by Jo Swerling and Herman J. Mankiewicz from an original story by Paul Gallico
Cinematographer: Rudolph Maté
Music: Leigh Harline
Cast: Gary Cooper (Lou Gehrig), Teresa Wright (Eleanor Gehrig), Babe Ruth (himself), Walter Brennan (Sam Blake)
Running Time: 128 minutes
Premiere: July 15, 1942, Astor Theater, New York

THEY GOT ME COVERED (1943)

Director: David Butler
Screenplay: Harry Kurnitz, from an original story by Leonard Ross and Leonard Spigelgass
Cinematographer: Rudolph Maté
Music: Leigh Harline; song "Palsy Walsy" by Harold Arlen and Johnny Mercer
Cast: Bob Hope (Robert Kittredge), Dorothy Lamour (Christine Hill), Lenore Aubert ("Mrs. Vanescu"), Otto Preminger (Fauscheim)
Running Time: 96 minutes
Premiere: March 4, 1943, Radio City Music Hall, New York

THE NORTH STAR (1943)
Rereleased as ARMORED ATTACK

Director: Lewis Milestone
Screenplay: Lillian Hellman
Cinematographer: James Wong Howe
Music: Aaron Copland; lyrics by Ira Gershwin; dances by David Lichine
Cast: Anne Baxter (Marina), Dana Andrews (Kolya), Walter Huston (Dr. Kurin), Walter Brennan (Karp)
Running Time: 106 minutes
Premiere: November 4, 1943, Victoria and Palace Theaters, New York

UP IN ARMS (1944)

Director: Elliott Nugent

Screenplay: Don Hartman, Allen Boretz, and Robert Pirosh, suggested by
    The Nervous Wreck by Owen Davis

Cinematographer: Ray Rennahan

Music: Louis Forbes

Cast: Danny Kaye (Danny Weems), Dinah Shore (Virginia), Dana Andrews
    (Joe), Constance Dowling (Mary Morgan)

Running Time: 105 minutes

Premiere: March 2, 1944, Radio City Music Hall, New York

THE PRINCESS AND THE PIRATE (1944)

Director: David Butler

Screenplay: Adapted by Don Hartman, Melville Shavelson, and Everett
    Freeman from a story by Sy Bartlett

Cinematographers: Victor Milner and William Snyder

Music: David Rose

Cast: Bob Hope (Sylvester Crosby), Virginia Mayo (Margaret Wasbrook),
    Walter Brennan (Featherhead), Walter Slezak (La Roche)

Running Time: 94 minutes

Premiere: February 9, 1945, Astor Theater, New York

WONDER MAN (1945)

Director: Bruce Humberstone

Screenplay: Arthur Sheekman, Don Hartman, Melville Shavelson, and
    Philip Ropp

Cinematographers: Victor Milner and William Snyder

Music: Louis Forbes; dances by John Wray; specialty numbers by Sylvia
    Fine

Cast: Danny Kaye (Edwin Dingle/Buzzy Bellew), Virginia Mayo (Ellen
    Shanley), Vera-Ellen (Midge Mellon), Donald Woods (Monte Rossen)

Running Time: 97 minutes

Premiere: June 8, 1945, Astor Theater, New York

THE KID FROM BROOKLYN (1946)

Director: Norman Z. McLeod

Screenplay: Adapted by Groves Jones, Frank Butler, and Richard Connell
    from the play *The Milky Way* by Lynn Root and Harry Clark; scenario
    by Don Hartman and Melville Shavelson

Cinematographer: Gregg Toland

Music: Carmen Dragon; music and lyrics by Jule Styne and Sammy Cahn;
    words and music of "Pavlova" by Sylvia Fine and Max Liebman

Cast: Danny Kaye (Burleigh Sullivan), Virginia Mayo (Polly Pringle), Vera-Ellen (Susie Sullivan)
Running Time: 113 minutes
Premiere: April 18, 1946, Astor Theater, New York

THE BEST YEARS OF OUR LIVES (1946)
Director: William Wyler
Screenplay: Robert E. Sherwood, from the verse novel *Glory For Me* by MacKinlay Kantor
Cinematographer: Gregg Toland
Music: Emil Newman
Cast: Myrna Loy (Milly Stephenson), Frederic March (Al Stephenson), Dana Andrews (Fred Derry), Teresa Wright (Peggy Stephenson), Virginia Mayo (Marie Derry), Harold Russell (Homer Parrish)
Running Time: 170 minutes
Premiere: November 21, 1946, Astor Theater, New York

THE SECRET LIFE OF WALTER MITTY (1947)
Director: Norman Z. McLeod
Screenplay: Ken Englund and Everett Freeman, adapted from the short story by James Thurber
Cinematographer: Lee Garmes
Music: David Raksin; songs by Sylvia Fine; musical director, Emil Newman
Cast: Danny Kaye (Walter Mitty), Virginia Mayo (Rosalind Van Hoorn), Boris Karloff (Dr. Hollingshead), Fay Bainter (Mrs. Mitty)
Running Time: 110 minutes
Premiere: August 14, 1947, Astor Theater, New York

THE BISHOP'S WIFE (1947)
Director: Henry Koster
Screenplay: Adapted by Robert E. Sherwood and Leonardo Bercovici from a story by Robert Nathan
Cinematographer: Gregg Toland
Music: Hugo Friedhofer and Emil Newman
Cast: Cary Grant (Dudley), Loretta Young (Julia Brougham), David Niven (Henry Brougham), Monty Wooley (Professor Wutheridge)
Running Time: 109 minutes
Premiere: December 9, 1947, Astor Theater, New York

A SONG IS BORN (1948)
Director: Howard Hawks
Screenplay: Harry Turgend, from the story "From A to Z" by Billy Wilder and Thomas Monroe

Cinematographer: Gregg Toland
Music: Emil Newman and Hugo Fiedhofer
Cast: Danny Kaye (Professor Hobart Frisbee), Virginia Mayo (Honey
    Swanson), Benny Goodman (Professor Magenbruch), Hugh Herbert
    (Professor Twingle)
Running Time: 113 minutes
Premiere: October 19, 1948, Astor Theater, New York

ENCHANTMENT (1948)
Director: Irving Reis
Screenplay: Adapted by John Patrick from the story "Take Three Tenses"
    by Rumer Godden
Cinematographer: Gregg Toland
Music: Emil Newman
Cast: David Niven (General Roland Dane), Teresa Wright (Lark Ingoldsby),
    Evelyn Keyes (Grizel Dane)
Running Time: 102 minutes
Premiere: December 25, 1948, Astor Theater, New York

ROSEANNA McCOY (1949)
Director: Irving Reis
Screenplay: Adapted by John Collier from a story by Alberta Hannum
Cinematographer: Lee Garmes
Music: Emil Newman
Cast: Farley Granger (Johnse Hatfield), Joan Evans (Rose McCoy), Charles
    Bickford (Devil Anse Hatfield), Raymond Massey (Old Randall
    McCoy)
Running Time: 100 minutes
Premiere: October 12, 1949, Capitol Theater, New York

MY FOOLISH HEART (1949)
Director: Mark Robson
Screenplay: Adapted by Julius and Philip Epstein from the story "Uncle
    Wiggily in Connecticut," by J. D. Salinger
Cinematographer: Lee Garmes
Music: Emil Newman
Cast: Dana Andrews (Walt Dreiser), Susan Hayward (Eloise Winters), Kent
    Smith (Lew Wengler), Lois Wheeler (Mary Jane)
Running Time: 98 minutes
Premiere: December 25, 1949, United Artists and Four Star Theaters, Los
    Angeles

OUR VERY OWN (1950)
Director: Dave Miller
Screenplay: F. Hugh Herbert
Cinematographer: Lee Garmes
Music: Victor Young
Cast: Ann Blyth (Gail), Farley Granger (Chuck), Joan Evans (Joan), Jane Wyatt (Lois Macaulay)
Running Time: 93 minutes
Premiere: July 27, 1950, Victoria Theater, New York

EDGE OF DOOM (1950)
Director: Mark Robson
Screenplay: Adapted by Philip Yordan from the story by Leo Brady
Cinematographer: Harry Stradling
Music: Emil Newman
Cast: Dana Andrews (Father Roth), Farley Granger (Martin Lynn)
Running Time: 99 minutes
Premiere: August 3, 1950, Astor Theater, New York

I WANT YOU (1951)
Director: Mark Robson
Screenplay: Adapted by Irwin Shaw from a story by Edward Newhouse
Cinematographer: Harry Stradling
Sound: Gordon Sawyer
Cast: Dana Andrews (Martin Greer), Dorothy McGuire (Nancy Greer), Farley Granger (Jack Greer)
Running Time: 102 minutes
Premiere: December 23, 1951, Criterion Theater, New York

HANS CHRISTIAN ANDERSEN (1952)
Director: Charles Vidor
Screenplay: Adapted by Moss Hart from a story by Myles Connolly
Cinematographer: Harry Stradling
Music: Walter Scharf; words and music by Frank Loesser; choreography by Roland Petit
Cast: Danny Kaye (Hans Christian Andersen), Farley Granger (Niels), Jeanmarie (Doro), Joey Walsh (Peter)
Running Time: 104 minutes
Premiere: November 25, 1952, Criterion and Paris Theaters, New York

GUYS AND DOLLS (1955)
Director: Joseph L. Mankiewicz
Screenplay: Joseph L. Mankiewicz, based on the play with book by Jo

Swerling and Abe Burrows, from the story "The Idylls of Sarah Brown," by Damon Runyon
Cinematographer: Harry Stradling
Music: Jay Blackton; music and lyrics by Frank Loesser; choreography by Michael Kidd
Cast: Marlon Brando (Sky Masterson), Jean Simmons (Sarah Brown), Frank Sinatra (Nathan Detroit), Vivian Blaine (Miss Adelaide)
Running Time: 150 minutes
Premiere: November 3, 1955, Capitol Theater, New York

PORGY AND BESS (1959)
Director: Otto Preminger
Screenplay: N. Richard Nash, based on the folk opera, with libretto by DuBose Heyward, from the play *Porgy*, by DuBose and Dorothy Heyward
Cinematographer: Leon Shamroy
Music: George Gershwin; lyrics by DuBose Heyward and Ira Gershwin; conducted by Andre Previn
Cast: Sidney Poitier (Porgy), Dorothy Dandridge (Bess), Sammy Davis, Jr. (Sportin' Life), Pearl Bailey (Maria)
Running Time: 146 minutes
Premiere: June 24, 1959, Warner Theater, New York

Index